Endorsements

Sometimes it takes a while to recognize that someone has a special ability to get us to believe in ourselves, to tie that belief to our highest ideals, and to discover our potential and realize. This ability also drives us one to believe "yes I can, I will ". Dr Arun Mittal is charismatic!! His command over language is phenomenal and capacity to connect examples with concepts is infectious which ultimately keeps you turning the pages.

Mukesh Khare, Deputy General Manager, State Bank of India

This is really a very inspiring and awakening journey through a series of some of the most apt stories and examples of successful people. Dr. Mittal has an art of presenting the essentials of success in a very lucid manner. The examples included in the book provide the reader with systematic clues for understanding the concepts formulae of success. This takes you to a level where you feel that success is possible for you as well. I believe that this all-encompassing book can enlighten the readers and guide them to achieve true success. I congratulate Dr. Mittal for this wonderful creation and recommend all readers to realize their dream of success by using the simple rules of success described here.

Dr. P. K. Sikdar, President, Intercontinental Consultants and Technocrats Pvt. Ltd and Former Professor, IIT Mumbai

Excellent! A truly readable book! This book is like a school of personality development, which encompasses many mantras of success in its 21 lessons. These mantras not only throw light on the various rules of personality development, but also enumerate the ways to implement them so as to make one's life a success. A thoroughly practical and knowledge-inspiring book.

Dr. S. L. Gupta, Dean, Waljat College of Applied Sciences, Muscat (An academic partner of Birla Institute of Technology, Mesra, Ranchi)

A book which explains many of the untouched topics of human behaviour, personality development and success in an extremely interesting, practical and extensive manner. It also contains the principles of goal-setting, and an analysis of the techniques involved in achieving them. Undoubtedly a readable and worth collecting book.

Dr. Nawal Kishor, Professor, School of Management Studies, Indira Gandhi National Open University (IGNOU)

Dr. Arun Mittal, in this book, has covered certain significant subjects with regard to achievement of success, which are not normally found in many self-help books. If you want to achieve success along with happiness, then this book is exclusively for you. This book not only deals with individual success, but gives directions for positive changes for the society. A book extremely useful for today's generation. An inspiring book written with great responsibility.

Dr. Munish Makkad, Director, Birla Institute of Technology, Mesra, Ranchi, Noida Campus

This book is a very innovative and practical guide to success for all those who wish to get success without sacrificing personal happiness. The content is inspiring as well as convincing. The most interesting aspect of the book is the part that includes the do's and don'ts of success. The mantras are simple but effective. I wish Dr. Mittal all the best for this excellent piece of work.

Prof. M. Ashraf Rizvi, former Professor IIM Indore, Director, Jaipuria Institute of Management, Lucknow

Finally, a self-help book that can actually be put to practise. A simple and practical book that is also interesting and inspiring. The rules are all supported by practical examples and anecdotes. Such a book becomes more important when written by a teacher who is in constant touch with young and intelligent youth of today. The messages are equally relevant to readers of all ages. Best wishes to Dr. Mittal for his effort.

Deepak Singhal, Chief Executive Officer, Silver Circle

In his debut venture, Dr. Arun Mittal talks about the simple ways to succeed in life. Interspersed with life-enriching short stories, the book gives an easy road-map for success. Significantly, each of the 21 chapters begins with a quote by a philosopher/thinker, whose meaning is then explained in detail through motivational text and educative stories. The book is meant not just for students and professionals, but for all those who want to lead a peaceful and comfortable life.

Rajkumari Tankha, Freelance Editor and Writer

I Can...
I Will...

From **'Knowing the things'**...
   to **'doing the things'**

Dr. Arun Mittal

STERLING PUBLISHERS PRIVATE LIMITED
Regd. Office: A-59, Okhla Industrial Area, Phase-II,
New Delhi-110020. CIN: U22110PB1964PTC002569
Tel: 26387070, 26386209; Fax: 91-11-26383788
E-mail: mail@sterlingpublishers.com
www.sterlingpublishers.com

I Can... I Will...
© 2015, Dr. Arun Mittal
ISBN 978 81 207 9889 2

All rights are reserved. No part of this publication may be reproduced, stored in a retrieval system or transmitted, in any form or by any means, mechanical, photocopying, recording or otherwise, without prior written permission of the original publisher.

PRINTED IN INDIA

Printed and Published by Sterling Publishers Pvt. Ltd., New Delhi-110 020.

Contents

	Acknowledgements	vi
	Preface	vii
1.	Take Initiative – Do Something New	1
2.	Positive Attitude	9
3.	Be Creative and Win the World	15
4.	Accept Change with the Passage of Time	23
5.	Set an Appropriate Goal for Your Life	29
6.	Make Practical Plans	35
7.	Turn Your Goal into Your Passion	41
8.	Become Result Oriented	47
9.	The Key to a Successful Plan Is Its Implementation	53
10.	Knowledge Is the Foundation of Success	61
11.	Communication – Make the Best of It	71
12.	Becoming an Expert in Business Communication	77
13.	Not Letting Your Self-Confidence to Be Shaken	89
14.	Common Sense – the Most Useful Element	95
15.	Knowing Your Personality	101
16.	Keep a Control over Your Emotions	113
17.	Manage Your Stress	121
18.	The Basic Mantra of Success – Time Management	129
19.	Be a Strong Person	139
20.	Avoid Enemies and Also Friends Who Betray	147
21.	Handling Criticism	153

Acknowledgements

I Can... I Will... is not only the result of my efforts. In my school days I had a keen interest in inspirational and spiritual books. My father **Sh. M. P. Mittal** made my efforts more fruitful by telling me the meaning and importance of those books in life. Instructive stories, proverbs, and inspiring tales narrated by him since my childhood impressed me a lot and changed my attitude towards life. In fact, his teachings are the foundation of this book.

Writing this book would have never been possible for me without the support of my wife **Megha** and son **Aarav**. **Megha** has not only given me enough time to work on the book but has also reviewed it critically and suggested changes with a valuable inclined. I cannot thank her enough for her contribution towards this book.

I want to express my sincere gratitude to my academic mentor **Dr. S. L. Gupta,** with whom I learned so many enriching things that benefited me for the subject matter of this book.

Also I thank my acquaintance **Mr. Arvind Joshi** and **Mrs. Ritambhara Dwivedi,** whose assistance helped tremendously in writing this book. I would also like to thank the eminent people from academia and industry who have provided great endorsements.

And let's not forget my wonderful teachers and students who have played such a major role in the learning process of my life.

Dr. Arun Mittal

Preface

This is a compilation, not only of ideas, but also of experiences. This is an era of cut throat competition where a practical approach is required at all times. The concepts and ideas also change with the passage of time. To achieve success in a changing environment, we need abilities and expertise which the Business world and the society perceives as our strengths. In this book, I have made an attempt to link knowledge, self-confidence, positive thinking, result oriented approach, and many other aspects of human behaviour, with the practical world. It took me 11 years to complete this book. In my childhood, I had heard a story which helped me a lot to change my way of thinking. Before saying anything more, I would like to narrate that story.

A rich businessman had four sons, all of whom were honest and diligent. The businessman was suffering from prolonged illness, and consequently used to worry regarding the selection of an appropriate successor who will look after the business after his death.

He asked his trusted manager regarding the action to be taken in this regard. The manager suggested that the successor should be one who was the most intelligent of all four and who possessed a new way of thinking.

The businessman thought about the idea and gave ten rupees to each to his four sons. While doing so, he showed them a room and told them that whoever filled the room by the articles bought with the ten rupees he had given, would be his successor.

After some time, the first son bought cotton worth ten rupees and tried to fill the room. The room filled to some extent, but not completely. Then, the second son brought dried fodder for ten rupees. This time also, the room could not be filled completely. After a few days, the third son bought scrap newspapers to fill the room, but he also was unsuccessful.

Ten days passed, but the youngest son did not return, and the businessman, his manager, and the three brothers kept waiting for him.

The youngest son appeared suddenly one day—empty-handed. Seeing him in that state, all the three brothers started laughing at him. The businessman asked, "What happened? You did not bring anything?" To this, he replied. "I have definitely brought something, but not after spending ten rupees, but rather one rupee, and this shall fill the whole room."

Hearing this, all were surprised and went into the room to see what he had brought.

The youngest son took out a candle and a matchbox from his pocket, placed the candle on the floor, and lit it. The whole room was filled with light.

Seeing his intelligence, the businessman, manager, and the three brothers were very happy. The manager said to the businessman, "You see, an ideal successor should be like this. He should not be in hurry while doing things, think in an unconventional manner, economize, and also finish the allotted work."

There is a Sanskrit saying, "One who is devoid of knowledge, does not give way alms, does not do austerities, does not have wisdom, does not have a pleasant nature, is without any quality and does not believe in dharma, such a person is a burden on earth, and is an animal in the garb of man". These qualities have been included in this book at some place of the other.

 This book not only puts forth an explanation to the essential theories, but also attempts explain them by examples, statements, arguments and stories. It also convinces the reader regarding a happier and more prosperous life after implementation of the theories given therein.

 The book not only tells "What to do", but also throws light on "How to do". This is an extremely important topic which is often ignored.

 I hope that this attempt of mine shall be liked by all the readers, and shall help in their personality development and achievement of success. I await your feedback and well wishes.

Website: www.arunmittal.com
blog: www.arunmittal.blogspot.com

Dr. Arun Mittal
Mobile: 9873957205
dr_arunmittal@yahoo.com

1
Take Initiative — Do Something New

Be the first one . . . to think different

Be the first one . . . to act different

Be the first one . . . to be different

Yes indeed! For a long-lasting success, be the first one to do anything. In business, it is called the "First Mover Advantage". The person who is initiates something new is known as a trendsetter. He or she is considered the expert in that particular field. Many business personalities take initiatives in their businesses before all others and their actions are then followed by the rest of the world. This can be explained with the help of the following example:

Who is the originator of the Six Sigma concept?

Most of the readers can answer this correctly. It is, of course, Bill Smith of Motorola. And we all are aware how utmost important this idea is. It describes the concept of quality and perfection. This is a real achievement, something original, innovative, creative, novel, and path breaking.

Many people can invent and conceive ideas. You must have heard about the book *Ethical Hacking*. Its author Ankit Fadia became the youngest author on this subject at fifteen years of age when his book was published by Macmillan India. He was not only innovative but dared to be the first one to think differently. Others could not conceive such an idea and even if they thought of anything like that, they never pursued or acted on it.

Not only in the field of business and technology, but in the social and spiritual fields also there are many great personalities who have taken initiatives and have become living legends. The best contemporary example is of Anna Hazare who led the movement against corruption in India. We all know about yoga, but Swami Ramdev has redefined it and made it popular on Indian television. His art of connecting spiritual and patriotic messages with yoga appeals to Indians.

Small Efforts Can Solve Big Problems

Mohan used to work as a clerk in a company. One day, his colleague Shyam appeared very disturbed as his son was very ill and he needed one lakh rupees within a week in order to save his son's life. To arrange this amount was an uphill task for Shyam. Everyone consoled him by offering lip sympathy, but no one actually offered material help.

Unfortunately, Mohan was not in a position to help Shyam. However, he was not ready to lose heart. After pondering over the problem, he finally chalked out a plan, and immediately got into action. He started writing emails to all his colleagues, requesting them to contribute money towards Shyam's son's treatment. He emailed to 100 colleagues, which included people who were superior, or lower or holding the same rank as him. Mohan appealed to each of them to donate at least Rs. 100 and also proposed to take similar action for any colleague in need in the future. He kept on interacting with all of them for one week trying unceasingly.

By the end of the week, he saw he had got a mixed response. He was astonished to see that some of them did not show any sympathy by not donating even a rupee, while others went beyond the Rs. 100 appeal and contributed 3 to 4 thousand rupees each. Finally, he was able to collect the targeted Rs. 1,00,000.

When Shyam received the money, he was really moved. He witnessed how the initiative taken by Mohan turned into a concrete result. Mohan had taken a small step, taken an initiative, and this small but great effort not only gave a new life to Shyam' son, but also set a precedent in the company, to join hands and collect funds to help any colleague in need.

> Any great task or outstanding invention is always because someone took initiative.

Benefits of Taking Initiative

- **Recognition:** Whenever you take an initiative, you establish a special identity and get noticed even in a large crowd. Dr. Kiran Mazumdar Shaw of Biocon

Limited, Water Man Rajendra Singh Magasaysay award winner, and Social Activist Anna Hazare are a few such examples.

- **Maximum Attention:** Initiators have a better image in the society and gain maximum public attention. When someone takes an initiative at the workplace, the boss will tend to trust him or her with jobs requiring maximum responsibility. The person's name will be etched in the boss's mind. The habit of taking initiative gains you more respect and opportunities in an organization.

- **Knowledge Enhancement and Personality Development:** Initiative teaches us a lot of good things. We willingly do something, accept the challenge, and start action much before everyone else. People become more curious to know about our success or failure. This makes us more dedicated towards the initiative taken and encourages us to put in maximum effort in order to be successful. During this entire process, we learn a lot, resulting in enhancement of knowledge and personality development.

- **Getting an edge over others:** After a while, you become habitual of taking initiative at any level, whether social or professional. This habit gives you an edge over friends and colleagues.

How to Develop the Habit of Taking Initiative

You need not necessarily have to prove yourself by taking up a mammoth task or being an innovator. You can begin by taking small initiatives in your daily routine. And very soon you get habitual of taking initiatives and get maximum benefits by availing the opportunities provided to you by the environment. I would quote a few examples of taking initiatives:

1. In a classroom situation, a teacher asks the students, "Who among you will give the first presentation?"

The student who raises his or her hand first is said to be taking an initiative. (Usually no one wants to be the first one and it is the teacher who has to decide).

2. Suppose, in an organization, the office timings are 9:00 to 5:30 and at 5:30, there is a usually a huge crowd of employees at the gate, waiting to get out. To avoid that rush, you decide to wait for another ten minutes and do something productive. During this period, you can plan for the next day or you can work on some report, walk in the open lawn, or do some stretching exercises to relieve your fatigue.

3. If you join your father's business and you find that there is no professional training provided to the employees, you can take up the initiative and introduce professional training for the employees in order to enhance their skills. You can start a Customer Service helpline for improving customer satisfaction. You can strengthen your business in technical aspects by taking various initiatives.

4. If you are a teacher, you can be the source of inspiration to your students. Teach something which is beneficial to them, even it is beyond their syllabus. Give them opportunities to develop their creative thinking, improve their general awareness, and make them morally sound.

Whenever we take initiative, we get an extra advantage and respect. On one hand we get self-satisfaction if we take initiative to do something for the society and on the other hand we achieve monetary benefits, admiration from our colleagues and boss, and appreciation from customers, if we take an initiative in our professional arena. Our habit of taking initiatives makes us different from others.

It takes the Navy three years to build a ship. It will take three hundred years to build a new tradition. The evacuation will continue.

ANDREW CUNNINGHAM

By now you must have understood the meaning of taking initiative. To appreciate this concept, just read the following story and see the magic of taking initiative:

The Story of Two Clerks

Once there was a rich, kind, and intelligent grain merchant by the name of Dhaniram who had a thriving business of purchasing and selling various types of grains. He used to purchase grain from farmers and sell it to flour mills, households, and retail shopkeepers. He was not only rich, he had a large heart too. He was very kind to all his employees—clerks and servants. He had two assistants to take care of his business—Kranti Kumar and Shanti Kumar. Kranti's salary was Rs. 10,000 and Shanti was getting 50,000. Kranti and Shanti both were hired about 5 years ago and, at that time, each was paid the same, that is, Rs. 5000. But at present salary of Shanti was 10 times, while Kranti's salary merely doubled. Due to this Kranti used to be very upset and frustrated. One day, he could not control his emotions and asked Dhaniram as to the reason his salary was so little compared to Shanti when both had the same designation and were doing the similar kind of work. Dhaniram replied that the salary difference was justified but Kranti was not convinced with the answer. Dhaniram promised to prove the same.

Then, Dhaniram saw a farmer standing with his tractor full of bags of grain. He asked Kranti to go and ask what grain the farmer was carrying in his tractor. Kranti went to the farmer, asked him and got back to Dhaniram and told him that the farmer was carrying rice. Dhaniram said, "Well done! Tell me, which place does he belong to?" Kranti thought for a while and replied, "But you never told me to ask this." Dhaniram nodded his head. Then he called Shanti, who was busy somewhere else, and asked him to find out what grain the farmer was carrying in his bags. Shanti went and came back after almost one hour, drenched in heavy sweat. Kranti was surprised to see this and said to Dhaniram, "See, he has taken almost an hour to let you know something which I told you in just few minutes." Dhaniram ignored this comment and asked Shanti about what the farmer was carrying. Shanti replied, "Sir, the farmer was carrying rice. He came from Dehradun in U.P., which is very famous for rice.

I asked him the rate and found it reasonable, still I settled the deal after proper negotiation." Dhaniram asked, "But you took so long and you are full of sweat. Why?" Shanti replied, "After finalizing the deal, I tried get the bags unloaded in our nearby store, but it was full and I also found that all the three other stores had no more storage space. I then went to our friend and neighbour Radheshyam, settled the rent for a month with him and unloaded the entire grain in one of his stores. On my way back from that store to our shop, I decided to come through the market area and informed a few of our retailers about the good rice we bought. Because I was in a rickshaw and sun was at its peak, that's why I am drenched in sweat." Dhaniram was very happy to see the commitment of Shanti and appreciated him for it. Then he looked at Kranti and asked, "Do you still have any question?" Kranti Kumar was quiet. Obviously, he had got his answer.

What did you learn from this story?
The lesson learnt is that we should not always do only as directed and when directed. To achieve an extraordinary performance, we need to take initiative and do certain things on our own. Only people who follow this approach do wonders in their respective fields.

> **Today, the corporate world does not need clerks, it needs managers who can take decisions by their own initiatives rather than always waiting to get directions from their boss.**

You do not do anything unique or different but you break the tradition and change the work culture. Initiatives always lead to the betterment of your own self, family, society and the entire world. Take the example of Dr. Kiran Bedi, the first woman IPS officer of India, who took many initiatives while being in service, such as traffic management, narcotics control, etc. She initiated many reforms in the management of prisons and undertook a number of measures such as detoxification programmes, Art of Living, Prison Courses, yoga, vipassana, meditation, redressing of complaints by prisoners, and literacy programmes. It is only because of taking initiatives that she could do something different from the other officers, which is remarkable in the history of Indian police.

Some Important Tips for Taking Initiatives

1. Always think positive (Read Lesson 2: Positive Attitude).
2. Be Optimistic—this is the first condition for taking initiatives.
3. Learn to sacrifice your personal interests for the benefit of your organization, society, and country.
4. Think about what can be done for the betterment of your organization in particular and the society in general. You will notice that the habit of taking initiative will automatically develop in you.
5. Start taking initiative with small things such as celebrating birthdays of grandparents and coordinating the celebration of festivals at your workplace. By doing such acts, you will learn to be responsible and will develop the habit of taking initiatives in your life.

> **Success Mantras are written in books, but only those people succeed who take initiative and implement these mantras.**

2
Positive Attitude

The first noticeable attribute of all extraordinary and successful people is their Positive Attitude

Positive Attitude, nowadays, is very common in discussion, but many people don't know its meaning. *"Positive attitude is simply finding out the best things even when you are in the worst circumstances."* In this era of cut throat competition and highly stressed world, we need to think positively about life; otherwise we will never be successful.

> **Failure is 99% Success
> Take it Positively**

Indeed, most of the times it is just one per cent less effort, or may be you were simply unfortunate in having missed success.

My lesson begins with a small story. The story presents the definition of positive attitude given in this lesson.

The Story of Buddhu and Shuddhu

There were two brothers—Buddhu and Shuddhu. Both were almost of the same age. Buddhu was plagued with negative attitude and always found negativity in everything. He could always detect something bad in everyone. At the same time, Shuddhu was bursting with positive attitude—the exact opposite of Buddhu. He would find positivity even in the most demanding situations. He was forever positive and happy.

Their mother was dismayed over the extreme behaviours of her children. She wanted them to have a balanced outlook. One day she conceived a plan. She placed a box of chocolates under Buddhu's (the negative boy) pillow thinking that once Buddhu woke up, he would be pleasantly surprised to find the box full of chocolates and it may result in changing his attitude. Simultaneously, she put some horse droppings in Shuddhu's bed so that he may encounter some negativity. Next morning, Buddhu sprang out of his bed and shouted, "Who has put chocolates here? Someone is really my enemy and wants me to eat these chocolates so that my teeth will rot and decay," and started quivering with anger.

When Shuddhu woke up and discovered horse droppings on his bed, he looked at them carefully and after pondering over a while, shouted with joy, "Horse droppings! Wow! It means there is some horse close by. That's great! I will get a chance to ride that horse today."

That is called an attitude! It may be positive or negative.

However, attitude can be changed though it requires a lot of time and effort. We shall dwell more upon building a positive attitude. Many a times we go through difficult stages in our lives. A positive attitude gives us immense power to face such a situation.

> **A person with positive attitude will find lotus in a mud pond, but a person with negative attitude will see a smudge even in the moon.**

Understanding positive attitude is very simple. Often we see two persons having two totally different approaches towards the same object. These approaches may show us negative and positive attitude.

Why Should We Have a Positive Attitude?

We face lot of challenges in our day to day life. We may get these challenges from our external world viz., our colleagues, bosses, juniors and seniors, or our family members, or others with whom we interact professionally or personally. At times, people do not come up to our expectations and we feel let down. A positive attitude helps us to get out of such situations.

Positive attitude is the first step towards success. Let's take the example of our Olympic medallist Yogeshwar Dutt, the wrestler who suffered a knee injury in 2006 but never gave up and emerged a winner by bagging a gold medal in the 2010 Commonwealth Games and a bronze in the 2012 London Olympics. Sachin Tendulkar, the batting maestro, faced serious injuries a number of times, including a Tennis elbow, in his 23 years long career, but because of his sheer grit and positive attitude, he faced the tough times and became the first batsman in the world to score 100 international centuries. Could this have been possible without a positive attitude?

How Can We Convert a Negative Attitude into a Positive One?

Let us learn the process of building a positive attitude with the help of an inspiring story.

Change in Hari's Attitude

There was once a life insurance advisor named Vishnu, who was very wise, conscientious, and a positive thinker. He was among the top performers in the company. Once his company decided to assign a rural territory to him because of very low sales response from those areas. Vishnu, during his first visit, met a villager named Hari, who was around 30 years old, and asked him to buy an insurance policy to secure his family's future. Hari straightaway refused and said, "There is a rule in our family that no one buys insurance." Vishnu was surprised and wanted to know the reason behind the rule. Hari explained that once his uncle, who was 30 years old, had purchased a life insurance policy and he died in a road accident just after 5 years of buying that policy. This led the family to believe that an insurance policy brought bad luck and never to buy it. Vishnu

Positive Attitude

was now clear about their mind block. He asked Hari to give him 5 minutes to explain the benefits of insurance, to which Hari agreed. Vishnu asked him if he had ever seen anyone else dying in an accident at the age of 35. Hari thought for a while, slowly nodded his head in affirmation and told Hari about his neighbour who had died at that age. Vishnu then asked Hari if that neighbour was insured. Hari said no.

Vishnu shot another question at Hari, asking him if that neighbour's family got any monetary help from any company or elsewhere. "Certainly no," Hari replied. Vishnu then wanted to know if Hari's uncle's family got any money after he died. Hari recalled that his uncle's family received Rs. 2,00,000 from the insurance company.

Vishnu, put his hand on Hari's shoulder and asked, "Now tell me which death was more painful—death with insurance or death without insurance?"

Hari understood the point. He accepted that his uncle's death was less painful because the money his family got as insurance claim was used for the marriage of one of his uncle's daughters. He thanked Vishnu for changing his illogical attitude towards life insurance.

> **Only a logical explanation can covert a negative attitude into a positive one.**

Try to recall the first scene of the Mahabharata war where Arjun, the great warrior, threw away his Gandeev (bow) and declared that he will not fight against his own family members. Arjun had his own logics behind his negativity. But Lord Krishna, an expert of *Karma*, wiped the negativity out of Arjun's mind. The table below discusses the reasoning given by Arjun to defend his negative attitude and the solutions to turn it into positive one given by Lord Krishna:

Converting a Negative Attitude into a Positive Attitude

Arjun's Dilemma	Krishna's Clarification
These all are my family members and relatives, I cannot fight with them.	No one is a family member or a relative in war. All are merely warriors.
What would I do without my Grandfather, Guru, and brothers even if I win? There is no use of such victory.	You are not fighting for victory, but to establish Dharma and to punish those who are doing injustice.
But why should I kill my Grandfather, Guru, or brothers, isn't it sinful?	Because they are supporting injustice.
But why this is happening to me only?	Because you are the greatest warrior of this era. Winning over injustice is your duty, you are a role model for the coming generations, you are the hope for those who seek justice. You are not fighting this war for yourself but for the society.

The logical reasoning presented by Lord Krishna convinced Arjun. He immediately picked up his Gandeev and blew his conch.

> A drunken husband knocked at the door of his house. His wife, carrying a broom to beat him, angrily opened the door. The husband responded in a very positive manner and asked, "Darling, why are you cleaning the house at such a late hour?"

3
Be Creative and Win the World

Creativity is allowing yourself to make mistakes.
Art is knowing which ones to keep.

SCOTT ADAMS

Creativity is one of the most beautiful gifts of God in the present times. In the business world, from production to marketing and advertising, creativity has a great role to play. Today, a whole lot of products are available in the markets which were unthinkable a few years ago. Many of the present scientific innovations were beyond the scope of human imagination earlier. This is because of creative thinking. Today's world is heavily dependent upon creative minds. And for this reason we need creative people in every field.

What is Creativity?

Creativity is the process of doing something new. It gives us the power to create something which is not so common. In simple words, creativity is the generation of a third idea with the help two different ideas. Thus, a generic definition of creativity can be presented as:

First object/Idea + Second object/Idea = Third object/Idea

Which means, when we combine two ideas, we get an entirely new idea. To understand the concept of creativity in depth, we would need to understand the western and Indian approach to creativity.

Western Approach

Western ideology defines creativity exactly in the same way which we discussed earlier. It recommends one to be creative by mixing two different ideas. For example, the discovery of a laptop would have been the result of combining a computer device with the mobility of human beings. The same would have been the case with mobile phones as well.

Let us assume that someone invents some specialized sensors to detect a drunk driver; the moment this inebriated person is behind the steering of a car, the sensors will ensure that the car does not start. These sensors are there to save people from drunk drivers. This is an example of creativity and someone must have added the two objectives as follows:

Drunk person + automatically stop the person from starting the car = Sensors capable of identifying the drunk person

By now, you probably understand the western approach to creativity.

Indian Approach

The Indian approach is based on the doctrine, **"We cannot create anything—neither any idea nor any object."** All the ideas are already present on this earth. We can only discover them. This can be explained with the help of a simple example. You consult a doctor for some disease. The Indian approach says that all the medicines and diagnosis are already present in the world. They existed prior to the knowledge of the doctor. In fact, it depends on the competence of the doctor to find the best medicine for you. And this is possible only when he or she is open to all the sources of information. This openness is the result of very high level of wisdom and extremely low level of ego.

Now the interpretation of the above gives us a **theory of creativity** which we have named as the **Ego-Wisdom theory**. This theory says that there are only two things in your mind— ego and wisdom, and both have an inverse relationship, which means that when one increases, the other decreases, and vice versa. We can understand this theory with the help of the following cases:

Category 1

100% Ego	No Wisdom

100% Ego, 0% Wisdom: People with only ego and no wisdom are considered to be the least creative ones because they believe that whatever they think is the best. They do not discuss their ideas with anyone and they feel insulted in seeking anyone's advice. A doctor with 100% ego and no wisdom will only believe in the medicines he or she has learned about and on the basis of his experiences with patients whom he has treated. The doctor will be 100% confident about the treatment' without reviewing the problem in much depth. This kind of doctor may be young or highly experienced.

Category 2

Ego (70%)	Wisdom (30%)

70% Ego, 30% Wisdom: In this state of mind, ego dominates wisdom and such a person's decisions are affected less by wisdom and more by ego. Such people consult others and might accept the views of those whom they consider superior in intelligence. The selection of people whom to take advice from is completely decided by them only. Other persons would have no value in their minds. Doctors with these traits in the earlier example will not carry out an in-depth analysis, nor will they refer to books other than the books they believe to be the best.

Category 3

Ego (50%)	Wisdom (50%)

50% Ego, 50% Wisdom: Such a combination of ego and wisdom is the most commonly observed one. These people usually are professionals like CAs, lawyers, and consultants, etc. Most doctors also fall into this category. This also includes salaried professionals like professors, engineers, and managers. These people are experts in their own fields. They consult and comply with the expert advice. They follow the written principles, results of experiments, test reports, etc. They abide by the verified results rather than their own knowledge. This habit makes them less egoistic and wiser.

In the example given, a doctor with these traits will believe on your test reports, historical data, etc., and if he or she finds any mismatch between their knowledge and the test reports, they will accept the reports instead of believing their own knowledge.

Category 4

Ego (30%)	Wisdom (70%)

30% Ego, 70% Wisdom: Such people are not very common, but they are considered to be the best kind of persons in the society. These people have attained excellence in life. They soak up knowledge from everywhere and use whatever is useful for them and also to the people around them. They are experienced people who go beyond logics and create new logics. For example, Sachin Tendulkar, Amitabh Bachchan, Birju Maharaj, Kishore Biyani, Asha Bhonsle are some of the persons who belong to this category. Such persons have very less ego and can think beyond the traditional tests, researches, reports, experiments, principles, and theories. They can easily accept the situation when something goes wrong. They also have the capacity to bounce back during bad times.

Sometimes, you may have noticed that a young doctor will advocate a particular medicine so strongly as if it was the only medicine which will cure the patient. But an experienced doctor will usually educate you with the pros and cons of the recommended medicine and also about any other possible treatments, in case that particular medicine fails to work. Such a doctor will give you a patient hearing and may even consult a junior doctor as well. He or she might also discuss the case with their fellow doctors, seniors, and anyone who can enable them to understand the disease in depth. This doctor can even suggest you some traditional treatments like Ayurvedic or Homeopathic, in spite of the fact that they are allopathic practitioners.

Category 5

Ego (0%)	Wisdom (100%)

0% Ego, 100% Wisdom: This is the rarest category — 100% wisdom is a very difficult and rare phenomenon. We seldom find such people. There are so many great personalities in the world, but they also do not seem evolved enough to belong to this category. The only name that comes to our minds is Lord Krishna. After reading Mahabharata, you will get to know that he had zero ego and was full of wisdom. In our example, only the doctors who have been involved in researching human body for a very long time — probably more than 50 years — will fall into this category. Such doctors never make tall claims about the efficacy of any medicine for some disease. They can accept any time that all the knowledge, experience, reports, facts, and clues could be false. Of course, it is rare to find such doctors.

> We know, there are many things, we don't know.
>
> **DONALD RUMSFELD**

Let us try to understand how people in this category behave with the help of the following story:

The Large-heartedness of Gautama Buddha

One day, Gautama Buddha was sitting in meditation and a little distance from there some children were throwing stones at mangoes hanging on a tree. By mistake, a stone hit Gautama Buddha, and he started bleeding from his forehead. However, Gautama Buddha was not disturbed and maintained his cool. The children got frightened, went to him and asked for forgiveness. Gautama Buddha said with utter humility, "Children, it is I who should beg for an apology."

On hearing this, the children were taken aback. One of them mustered courage to ask the reason for this, to which Gautama Buddha replied, "Because when you hit the tree, it gave back fruits to you, but when you hit me, I could not give anything to you. I am not good like that tree." The children were surprised to see the large-heartedness of Gautama Buddha.

This type of a person belongs to Category 5. These people are very rare and often not considered practical by the society.

How to Be Creative

To be creative you can adopt any one or both of the approaches (western/Indian). The most important thing we need to be creative is openness of mind to ensure acceptance of new thoughts and ideas. Concentrating on following points can increase your creativity multiple number of times:

Steps to Become Creative

- Think different and dare to execute.
- Be patient—listen to others' views, test them. Maybe you can do something new by combining others' views and your own capabilities.
- Try to be in the fourth stage of the Ego-Wisdom theory.
- Make unusual combinations of different things.
- Experiment; some of your experiments will succeed one day, for sure.
- Challenge. It forms the basis to be more creative.
- Do not ever hesitate in doing something new.

> **Imagination is the beginning of creation. You imagine what you desire, you will be what you imagine, and at last, you create what you will.**
>
> **GEORGE BERNARD SHAW**

4
Accept Change with the Passage of Time

There is nothing permanent except *change.*

Time always flows at its own pace and things keep on changing. We are unable to keep a record of everything. However, it is a fact that the key to success is to adjust with the changing times. If we look through history, it will be evident that there were many companies which ruled the business world at one point of time, but they do not exist anymore. There is just one reason for this – that these companies could not keep up with the pace of change with time.

Humans have to change according to time, not only in their profession, but also in their personal life. Today is the age of technology and those who are not technically competent are bound to lag behind. In order to change, we have to train ourselves. This training helps us to replace our old manner of thinking to a new style of thought process.

How to Recognize Change?

Change never occurs abruptly, but happens rather gradually. It has got many forms and it is essential to recognize them.

Change in the organization and personality at the commercial level

There existed a time when appearances had no value and only knowledge was valued. But now the times have changed. Not only knowledge is valued by people, but your dress, manner of talking, and many other things are taken into account to judge your personality. I call this as **Content-Container Theory.**

"Content" implies material, while "Container" implies the thing in which the material has been kept. Which one is more important for you–content or container?

Many people will respond, "Content!"

Does that mean that the container is not significant at all? Do you purchase any item from the market which carries bad packaging? Definitely not. In today's world, content and container are both equally important. All people are attracted towards beautiful buildings, gifts wrapped in colourful paper, festive decorations, and good dresses. Often, we tend to purchase an item which carries an attractive packaging. The importance of show and packaging cannot be ignored today.

Here is a story on this subject.

The Indifference towards Change

A very old company, engaged in manufacturing steel trunks, was about to get a huge order from another company manufacturing edible products. In order to finalize the order, the production manager of the edible products company, Prabuddha Shah, visited the trunk manufacturing company. He was forced to park his car at a distance, as the head office of the trunk company was inside a very narrow lane. Somehow, he managed to reach the owner of the company.

He noticed a peculiar, blue coloured design on the wall behind the owner's chair. However, he did not pay much heed to it. He asked the owner if he could see the printouts of the requirements sent through email.

The owner replied that he did not know how to use the internet and the employee who operated the computer was on leave that day. Prabuddha was somewhat surprised, but then he took out his own laptop, and transferred the files into a pen-drive, and said, "No problem, the material is in this pen-drive. Please get a print of it."

The trunk company owner sent his peon for taking out the print. He came back after half an hour. Till then, Prabuddha kept glancing at his wrist watch, as he was losing precious time. When he asked about the reason for delay in getting the print, he was told that the material was of 125 pages, and their printer could not print more than 20–25 pages at a time. Hence, the printer had to be switched off repeatedly and cooled and that was the reason for delay.

Anyway, Prabuddha somehow took the matter further, and started discussing with the owner about the size and design of the trunk. Suddenly, the trunk company owner's pen stopped working. He jerked it on the wall behind him, and some ink drops splashed all over the wall. Only then could Prabuddha understand the mystery behind the peculiar blue design on the wall. He collected his laptop and without uttering a word, left the place.

What do we learn from this story?
1. In our business, we must include the latest methods of communication and technology.
2. Being indifferent towards change can lessen our chances of progress.
3. In the business world, sticking to the old style is liable to create a bad impression and in the long run, it is going to be extremely harmful.

Some persons find themselves unable to change in the world of business, and keep on regressing. Such people are often found saying:
- # At this age, it is not possible for me to learn the computer.
- # My age for education has long gone.
- # Why do I need to learn driving? If needed, I will hire a taxi.
- # The type of clothes you wear is not important; it is important to have brains.
- # I have spent my life like this so far. Whatever remains shall be spent in the same manner.
- # I do not use a mobile phone. It is a childish thing.

Such persons not only keep themselves away from modern gadgets, but also ask their colleagues to avoid them. If you have such people in your office, would you like to make friends with them? Such persons are always full of with pessimism. They also suffer from an inferiority complex and keep on cribbing about not knowing things which their bosses, colleagues, and juniors know about.

Change in Personality at the Individual Level

Individual level implies a change of behaviour, with the passage of time, with your family, children, and relatives. The youth today is unable to cope with the value systems of their elders. One reason for this is that elders, too, are unable to come down to the level of youngsters, and cannot relate with them.

For becoming a successful person, we have to necessarily change with time. Just ponder over this — Why are the people from the film industry proficient in so many languages? They learn new styles of dancing, singing, and many more things for many years before they are able to attain the status of a superstar. And what do they do when their stardom starts receding, their films earning lesser revenue, and they are unable to get advertisement assignments? They no longer do films, but start acting on the small screen and impart training to younger artists. This can be an example of their recognition of change with the advent of time.

> **Change is a type of risk that brings challenges and opportunities. It is a challenge for those who are unable to change according with time and an opportunity for those who adjust to the times.**

For bringing a change at the individual level, it is imperative that we come out of our comfort zone. Till we are not able to do this, we shall not be able to accept change. While learning about change from others, shed off your ego and, for a while, dump your old thoughts at the back of your brain.

Let us learn this concept more deeply through a story.

The Story of the Butterfly and the Housefly

Once, a butterfly lived in a garden. The entire day, it would buzz over the flowers and be happy with their fragrance. She became friends with a housefly who lived just outside the garden. Though the housefly was nice, but it used to dwell in cow dung. The butterfly did not like this and always attempted to convince the housefly to come over to the garden and enjoy the sweet fragrance of flowers. But the housefly's world was the cow dung. It did not believe that there was anything like a flower on this earth. It was contented with living on the cow dung.

One day, on the butterfly's insistence, the housefly gave in to the invitation, and agreed to visit the garden. However, while roaming in the garden, the expression on the housefly's face remained unchanged. Seeing this, the butterfly asked, "What is it, you do not seem to like the fragrance of the flowers?" To this, the housefly replied, "What fragrance? I smell the cow dung even here!" The butterfly was taken aback. It took the housefly to a marigold flower, and said, "Smell it, and you shall get fragrance." The housefly smelt the flower, laughed, and said, "Why do you fool me? It smells exactly like cow dung."

The butterfly was surprised. It made the housefly smell many flowers, but every time the housefly said that they all smelt like cow dung. At last, the butterfly took the housefly to a rose flower, and asked it to smell the rose. To this also, the housefly's reply was unchanged. This butterfly could not take it anymore. It pondered for a while, and asked the housefly to show its nose. The butterfly examined the nose of the housefly and said," You fool; your nose is smeared with dung. How can you smell the fragrance of flowers?!"

The same is the case with those who say they are ready for change, but do not want to change their old ways.

5

Set an Appropriate Goal for Your Life

Life without an aim is like a ship in the sea without a destination.

What is your aim in life? This is probably the most common question posed to every student by his or her schoolteacher or college professor. This question is also put to those who have reached a certain level of age but are still not settled in their lives. Usually people give a very unclear and vague answer to this question, saying, "I want to become a successful person."

What kind of a successful person?

In which field? What is the level of desired success?

And, in how much time?

Many of us will not have the answers to these questions and this poses the biggest challenge while deciding the goal of our life.

Yes! Being successful is the goal of everyone. Sachin Tendulkar, Amitabh Bachchan, Lata Mangeshkar, Kishore Biyani, Pandit Jasraj, Dr. A.P.J. Abdul Kalam, Amratya Sen, Chetan Bhagat are all successful people. But do you think all of them have put in similar efforts to be successful? Did all of them achieve success at the same age? Are their earnings similar? No, because they all belong to different fields. Similarly, you also need to select your own field so that you can steer your efforts in the right direction. At every step, we are all investing each moment of our life in achieving "our goal'".

Your Aim is Only Yours

A very important thing about your goal is that it should be your own goal. You may have seen the famous movie *Three Idiots*, in which the character Farhan (R. Madhvan) did not want to become an engineer. He wanted to become a wildlife photographer, but his father forced him to become an engineer. Ultimately, with the help of his friends, he collected the courage to tell his father about his preferred aim in life and successfully proved himself. Because being a wildlife photographer was his "own" aim.

What do you learn from this story?

Always decide your goal yourself.

Listen you your heart, it is on the left side, but it is always right!

Clearly say "No" to the goal which is not meant for you. Do not hesitate and waste time.

While deciding your goal, even a small mistake can make your life difficult.

What Is a Goal or Aim?

The definition of a goal helps us in selecting the goal of life. I define it as:

Your aim in life is *what your heart likes* **to do and also what your** *soul accept.* **You can** *do anything* **to get to that goal—something for which you can put in unconditional** *hard work* **with** *persistent efforts* **which never stop** *until you have achieved* **the goal.**

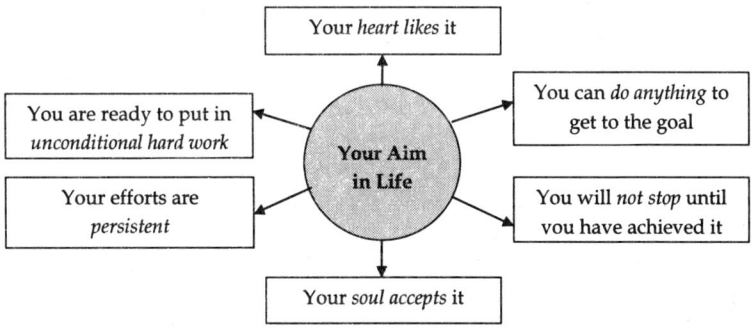

The Time to Decide and Achieve Your Goal

Deciding and achieving a correct goal is not a one-day task. Writing this book was one of my goals. I decided it when I was in school and I could achieve it only after tireless efforts of almost 11 years. In these 11 years, I read many books, attended hundreds of seminars and conferences, learned from experts, and devoted a lot of time in preparing the best subject matter.

> Don't let anyone else decide about your goal. This is like dumping your happiness in the deep dark box

What Is My Goal?

In addition, your goal is also decided by your strengths. We do **SWOT analysis** for this. SWOT stands for Strengths, Weaknesses, Opportunities, and Threats. Strengths and weaknesses are within a person and opportunities and threats are the components of the external environment. Lets understand about the importance of 'strength' in goal setting with the help of the following story:

Arjun: Gearing to Aim

Everyone knows about the great archer, Arjun from Mahabharat and his skills. He was the favourite disciple of Guru Dronacharaya. He had a single focus, that is, archery.

One day, Guru Dronacharya was awakened by the sound of someone practicing archery. He saw Arjun practicing in pitch darkness, and noticed that his arrows were hitting the target accurately. Seeing this, the Guru was astonished, as he had not taught Arjun the art of striking the target in darkness. He praised Arjun and asked, "Son, I never taught this to you, but how did you acquire this skill?" Arjun replied, "Yesterday, while having my meals, it was very dark inside the room. Even then, the morsel of food was reaching straight into my mouth, and nowhere else, as the hand is well aware where the mouth is located. The same way, I want that my arrow should find its target." Hearing this, the Guru was extremely pleased, and blessed Arjun that he may become a great archer.

The five Pandavs, in order to become warriors, chose their individual fields as per their capabilities. Arjun was blessed with a superior power of concentration, so he chose archery. Yudhisthir

Set an Appropriate Goal for Your Life

was the eldest, with extremely calm disposition who preferred war only for self-defence, and hence he decided to master the spear. Bheem was endowed with a strong body so he opted for "Gadaa" fighting. Nakul and Sahdev were extremely flexible, and therefore they chose the sword as their companion.

In fact, no one is best at everything. But if you decided your aim based on your strengths and tirelessly practiced and worked hard to achieve the same, you can be the best in your particular field.

Your strengths help you to decide your goal. If you are good in communication, you can become a motivational speaker or a Trainer. If you are physically fit and sound, you can think of being a sportsperson. If you have sound general knowledge, then you can embrace civil services. If you know the art of getting things done from others, you can be a successful manager.

One person may possess more than one core strength also. He or she can decide their aim in life based upon the mixture of those strengths. You must have observed that, many times, lawyer-parents have children opting for law as a profession, teachers' children might get into teaching, and businesspersons' children may take up business. Why? Because that's their strength; they had been learning it for long through their parents and grandparents.

However it is not mandatory that you always choose your parents' profession. You can prepare a list of your strengths and weaknesses. Everyone has some weaknesses along with certain strengths. But listing the weaknesses should not result in you developing an inferiority complex. When you wish to achieve something and some of your weaknesses are proving to be obstacles, you can remove the obstacles and move on. But, ultimately, you need to understand this practically about how early and how easily you can handle such weaknesses.

Opportunity is a very important word. It means, "Whatever you want to be, would it have great scope?" Today, the corporate and social world is so much developed that, from Humanities to Sciences, and from physical skills-based to mental skills-based fields, all of them give you an opportunity to showcase your talent and make a career. You just need to look for those opportunities and prepare yourself accordingly so that you can convert your passion into your profession.

The last step of SWOT is "Threats", which means the challenges from the environment. Threats are everywhere and you cannot be devoid of them. You will have to face them, using your talent and hard work. These threats will make you feel proud about achieving your goal.

So far you have understood the importance of aim in life and the factors to be considered while deciding it. In the next few chapters we will discuss about the policies, procedures, and methods to achieve one's goal.

> **I have only one aim in my life—
> Deciding the aim of my life!**

6
Make Practical Plans

90% of the plans are never implemented because they are made in the imaginary world rather than in the real world.

We make plans for performing tasks. Any task which is performed in a systematic manner leads to its successful completion. However, there is a big difference between an Ordinary Plan and an Effective Plan. An ordinary plan is limited to documentation only, hence it may also be referred as a "Paper Plan", but an Effective Plan is a practical plan. The difference between the two can be understood in the following manner:

Paper Plan	Practical Plan
Inspired by imagination. The planner remains in an imaginary world and sketches an ideal picture for all situations.	Inspired by the real world. The planner remains in the real world and sketches a practical picture in for situations.
The plan is mainly for display to others, get praise, and false gratification of self.	This plan is for implementation.
Such a plan is often made by those who consider making plans as their sole objective of life.	Such a plan is made by those who really want to achieve their objectives.
Such plans and their outcome are pleasant to look at, but when carried out, they produce equally bad and unpleasant results.	Such plans and their outcome appear ordinary and cumbersome, but when carried out, they produce good and logical results.
Such plans mostly remain limited to paper.	Such plans are definitely workable.

Practical Planning of the Sly Fox

In a jungle, there lived a fox couple along with their three children. In the same jungle, there lived a lion, who was very old. The lion lived near the place where the fox family lived and used to sit at the nearby pond. When any animal came to drink water at the pond, the old lion would catch and eat it. Hence, all the animals were scared to come near the pond.

One day, dad-fox and mom-fox could not manage to arrange water for their children. All of them were extremely thirsty. Mom-fox told dad-fox that they would have to go to the pond to drink water and also fetch it for the children, so he should make a plan to fool the lion.

Hearing this, dad-fox started to boast, "Yes, why not. To fool the lion in order to drink water, I have got one hundred plans in my mind." Hearing this, the mom-fox said, "Very well, then the problem is solved. In any case, I also have a plan in my mind." Hearing this, the dad-fox retorted, "What good can your single plan do? I have got one hundred plans." Mom-fox then said, "Wonderful, you go and fetch water for all of us, and also drink yourself to your satisfaction." Hearing this, dad-fox got nervous. He, in fact, feared the lion very much, and actually all his plans were absolutely theoretical. He said, "Oh no, I might get bored while walking such a long way, why don't you also come along with me?" Mom-fox immediately understood that all the hundred plans of dad-fox were practically useless. But she also had a plan in her mind and she was pretty confident regarding its success. Hence, both of them gave the necessary instructions to their children and went to get the water.

After covering half the way, the dad-fox started getting more and more scared of the lion. So the mom-fox told him, "I hope you remember your one hundred plans." Nervously, the dad-fox replied, "One hundred . . . no . . . I remember only fifty." After travelling further, the mom-fox asked again, "I hope you remember your fifty plans." The dad-fox was already trembling with fear by the mere thought of being near the lion. He said, "No, not fifty . . . but I remember twenty-five." When the pond and the lion were both in sight, the mom-fox asked again, "Now that we have reached near the pond and the lion, do you remember your twenty-five plans?" The dad-fox now started trembling very much, and said, "I do not remember any plan. Run for your life—I will not go near the lion!" Seeing the dad-fox terrified, the mom-fox said, "OK, I have a plan to deal with the lion. For that, you move away and hide behind hillock, while I will go and talk to the lion."

With a bowed head, the mom-fox went to the lion and spoke in an extremely humble tone,"Jeth Ji (elder brother of husband), right now I am in an extremely difficult situation and have come to seek your help." The lion liked the salutation of the mom-fox very much. He thought of luring her near to him by sweet words, so that when he attacked her, she would not be able to escape. And, as it is, there was no harm in listening to her words. Addressing the mom-fox, the lion said, "Tell me, sister, how can I help you?" The mom-fox replied, "I have had a quarrel with my husband and now we have decided to separate. We have three children. My husband says that he will keep two children with him, while I say that it is I who will keep two children. If you kindly decide on the matter, I shall be highly grateful."

Hearing about the young children of the fox couple, the lion's mouth started watering. He had not eaten tender meat since long. He said, "Sister, no issue. I shall make the decision; but I will be unable to decide without seeing the children first. You bring your children as well as your husband." The mom-fox started sensing the success of her plan. She said, "I will bring them right away. But, I have already travelled a long way and I am terribly thirsty. If you kindly permit me, I would like to drink some water and carry some for the way back."

The lion was still absorbed in the thoughts of the children and straightway gave his consent. The mom-fox drank water to her full satisfaction and also filled the pitcher she had brought with her. Thereafter, she went back home comfortably with her husband.

Points to Be Borne in Mind While Making Practical Plans

Any plan proves to be practical only when all important points are included in it. While preparing an effective and practical plan, five points are to be borne in mind.

Make Practical Plans

Time	Will I have sufficient time to execute the work I intend to do, in the manner I intend to do? Will the work be done within the stipulated time as planned?
Energy and Funds	For the proposed work, do I have sufficient funds and energy? Can I use the available funds and energy in a better way? If yes, use these in a better way and hence make another plan.
Work-life balance	What will be the effect of this plan on my work-life balance? Am I sacrificing my family time for the work or work-time for the family?
Aim of life	Does this plan differ from my life plan or aim? If yes, then it is foolish to invest energy, money, and time into it. Often, many persons from the corporate world come to me and express their intention to do Ph.D. I normally ask them, "Why? Do you intend to enter into the field of teaching?" They reply in the negative and say that they simply wish to prefix "Dr." to their name. A work or plan which does not coincide with your aims is not worth considering for investment of time and energy.
Possibility of success	What are the chances of success for the plan we are making for the work? This is extremely important to know as life is not a mere gamble or lottery, but something to be dealt with in a very systematic manner.

One can prepare a practical and effective plan, only when one bears the above points in mind.

Theoretical Plan of a Casual Writer

There was a newly-married writer. He rented a house and started living in it with his wife. His routine was to go out of the house in the morning and come back in the evening. After one month, the landlord approached his wife for the rent. In the evening, the wife informed the husband about it, to which he very coolly replied, "Tell him, whenever I get the royalty, I will pay the rent." The wife was convinced and when the landlord came again to ask for the rent, she gave him the same answer as instructed by the husband.

Nothing happened for one week. After one week, the landlord came again and the informed her husband. The writer once again replied, "As and when I get the royalty, I will pay." The wife thought that the royalty was to arrive within a day or two and so was fully convinced about the reply.

A fortnight passed and nothing happened. So when the landlord came this time, he asked for the money very angrily. The wife, in turn, asked the husband angrily about it. This time also, the writer replied, "O my beloved, why do you get angry? As and when I get the royalty, I will pay." This time, the wife angrily asked him, "And when are you going to get that royalty?" The writer replied casually, "Well, it is so simple. First of all, I must get into a mood to write something. Then I will start writing a novel. Then my novel will get finished. After that, I will search for a good publisher. Then, my novel will get published, and come into the market, and the sales will start. Then, my publisher will give me money at the end of the financial year. The moment I get the royalty, I will pay the rent!"

> **We must not only avoid making paper plans ourselves, but also keep those persons away from us who have the tendency of making paper plans.**

7
Turn Your Goal into Your Passion

The way an engine pulls a train to the destination, your passion also pulls you to your goal.

In Chapter 5, we discussed about selecting a goal. But how to attain that goal? This is possible only when it becomes your passion. It becomes your passion when you **keep thinking about it, working on it, and planning for it** only during your waking hours, sleeping hours, and even while moving around. There are a lot of differences between preparing to attain the goal **without any passion** and to prepare to attain it **with passion**. The differences are:

Person with a goal, without passion (A)	Person with a goal, with passion (B)
I must perform this work so that I attain my goal. God help me in removing obstacles, if any.	I shall perform this work, no matter what — even if the earth moves.
If I get help from that person, maybe this work will get slightly easier.	I can do this work all by myself, whether I get any help or not.
This work can always be done tomorrow. I can do some other work today.	I shall not do anything else till I am able to reach my goal.
Let me do some other work for a few days. This will benefit me a lot.	I have only one goal. I am not going to be swayed by any benefit, even for a moment.
My resources are depleting. Nobody is helping me. It seems that I have to change my goal.	My resources are depleting. Nobody is helping me. *There is no question of giving up now. It shall be much more challenging to attain the goal now.*
Why did I set a goal like this? I am neither able to attain it, nor utilize my energies elsewhere. It would have been better if I not have set this goal at all.	It is good that I set a goal so that I am saved from being directionless. Now I am confident that I am able to focus my energies on the right path.

Go through the above analysis carefully and ponder over it. What types of thoughts come to your mind? Are they from Column A or Column B? In case they are from Column A, you should realize that these arise due to a lessened passion towards the goal. What was the goal of our freedom fighters? Independence. They sacrificed their lives, took the blows and bullets of the British army on themselves. But, did their passion get any lesser? No! Had it lessened, we would have been slaves even today. Those who seek their goal never look back, and do not care about the difficulties which come in their way.

> **It is only when we deviate from our goal that we start seeing the difficulties in our path.**

When you start from home for office and face a red traffic light on the way, what do you do? You stop for a few moments. When the light turns green, you proceed further on the same road. Do you think:

1. Oh, there is red light in front of me. Left turn is free; I should move over there.

2. If I get any red signal on way to office, I will return and come back home.

3. Let me turn to the highway. There is no problem of red lights over there.

Just consider, if you start thinking on these lines, will you be able to reach your office at all? You do not mistake these mistakes and reach office on time. You face the red lights, traffic jams, and bumpy roads and if you have a flat tyre, you also commute by public transport but, in any case, you reach office. If you can toil so hard for a routine, daily work, can you not do the same for achieving the goal of your life? When you are not ready to compromise by changing your route to the office, then, how can you alter the course of your life or its desired route?

The famous Urdu poet, Bashir Badr has aptly said:
*Jis din se chala hoon, meri manzil pe nazar hai
Aankhon ne kabhi, meel ka paththar naheen dekha*
(From the day I started, I have my eyes on the destination; they have never noticed the milestone)

Abraham Lincoln was raised in extreme poverty, lost many elections, but finally became the President of the United States of America, which was his passion. Everyone is aware that the voice of Amitabh Bachchan; at one time, he was rejected by All India Radio during an audition test but the fact is that millions of people are fans of his magical voice.

Obstacles are not hurdles in achieving a goal. Rather, they test if you have the passion for your goal. If the passion is present, you do not need any support. If you are determined, the obstacles get scared and move away from you. Let us understand the actual meaning of passion from the next story:–

The First Lady Pilot without Hands

If you do not have hands, what type of work can you do? In such a situation, you will only think about the work you cannot do. But Jessica Cox is an exception. She is a girl from Arizona (U.S.A.) and was born without hands. She, by way of sheer grit, was able to obtain a pilot's licence at the age of 25, and thus became the world's first lady pilot without hands. Not only that, she also became the first woman to obtain a black belt in Tae-Kwon-Do.

Jessica admits, "I never say that I cannot do a thing; I only say that I have not tried doing it till now." Today, Jessica has two black belts in Tae-Kwon-Do. She does almost any kind of work done by hands, using her feet. She can drive, type on the keyboard, and is a licensed scuba diver. In her list of tasks, she has some more achievements such as tying her hair with a rubber band and climbing a mountain. Jessica has received a bachelor's degree in psychology from Arizona University. She is a motivational speaker and has lectured in around 17 countries.

Now answer the following questions:
1. Can the achievements of Jessica be termed as ordinary?
2. Did Jessica achieve whatever she did, without having passion?
3. Is any difficult goal possible without having a passion?

Just as a railway engine pulls a train, in the same way your passion drives you to your goal. In today's business world, the word passion has become an essential term. While facing an interview board, when you are asked about your goal, it is not only observed how clear you are about your goal, but also the amount of enthusiasm, happiness and positivity you have while discussing that goal. If you respond unenthusiastically, it is presumed that you have determined your goal all right, but you do not have the required passion for it inside you, and that you can deflect from your path any time.

When Does Your Goal Transform into a Passion?

Your goal does not remain just a goal, but turns into a passion, under these circumstances:
1. When you have fixed your goal using your heart. You consider the goal as a part of your own existence and cannot even think of your life without it.
2. When you do not have any other option. When your prestige, life, and a lot of money is at stake and you cannot afford to lose them.
3. When you wish to prove to the world that you can do a deed considered impossible. Or, when you wish to show something to a person who has let you down sometime in the past.

Then, in these circumstances, you give adequate importance to your desire to achieve and your goal becomes your passion.

> A dream is not the one which you see while you are asleep. It is the one which does not let you sleep at all.

How Can You Build Passion in Yourself?

To build a passion inside us, we have to develop our thinking in the direction of the passion itself. There are three types of people in this world:

Those who do some unusual work.

Those who witness some unusual work being done.

Those who do not know at all what is being done.

Which category would you like to fall into? If you are in the first category, then you need a passion of the highest degree, because you are going to do something unusual. A goal should be such which, when even imagined to be achieved, should fill enthusiasm inside you. For instance, your goal is to become an IAS officer and one day you are not in a mood to study for the competitive examination. At that moment, you start imagining about what will happen when you become an officer. You think of the amount of pride your friends and relatives will have in you. You will have a stature of your own. Your status will change from that of an ordinary person to that of a special person. The moment you envision such a scene in your mind, you will immediately get back to the preparation for the examination.

Always realize that you are not born just to pass your lifetime idly, but to do something which others may remember for ever. Everyone should quote your example of being the best in your field. Excellence does not come with ordinary efforts. For this, you will necessarily have to keep on trying. Only this feeling can produce a passion inside your mind.

Keep a close eye on your goal at every moment and watch if you are proceeding on the right path or not. The moment you gain some success in achieving your goal, do celebrate it as this will boost your enthusiasm.

Have confidence in your inner self. If you can think of a goal, you can achieve it. Always remember that the moment you start doubting your capabilities, your enthusiasm will begin to lessen, and your goal will fail to turn into your passion.

8
Become Result Oriented

Being result oriented means not just making efforts, but fighting it out till the goal is reached.

Result Oriented Approach

Throughout our lives, we keep on trying hard to do something. But often, we don't become successful despite trying repeatedly. Many of us remain content, thinking that at least we tried hard. In today's era of competition, it is extremely harmful to carry such a belief. An effort that does not produce a result has no meaning at all.

Having a result oriented approach means working with an approach in which attainment of the goal is of supreme importance. Whenever you face a hurdle in the path of your goal, you do not make any excuses. Rather, you start searching for an alternate path, and do not stop until you reach the goal.

You can well imagine that, when Hanuman Ji was unable to recognize the Sanjeevani Booti, (medicine that could make a dead person alive if used timely), he could easily have returned empty handed, and could have said to Lord Ram, "Forgive me, Lord, I could not recognize the Booti, so I have come back without it." But if he had said this, what would have been the consequences? The fact is that he did not give up his goal. Rather, he searched for an alternative and took the whole mountain, so that *Vaidya Sushen* (doctor of that time) could identify the *Booti* and save the life of *Lakshman*. This is truly a result oriented approach.

Importance of Result Oriented Approach

Let us try to understand the importance of this approach through a story.

Result Oriented Approach

Two people, namely Mahesh and Suresh, were employed by an insurance company as Sales Officers. Mahesh was well-versed in the art of communication, and had a large circle of friends. Also, he was smarter and had a better technical knowledge than Suresh.

The company assigned both of them the task of selling 10 policies each. This task was to be completed within one month. Both Mahesh and Suresh started off on the job.

After one month, their Branch Manager called both of them and asked them to give out the details of their sales.

Mahesh, had puffed and reddened eyes, and looked sleepy, while Suresh looked absolutely composed and cheerful. Mahesh said, "This was an uphill task for me, but I tried my best, and could not sleep peacefully for the whole month. I was busy throughout with my laptop and telephone. During this period, I called up 300 people, sent them e-mails, and tried to sell them policies. I toiled day and night." The Branch Manager said, "Very good, I expected this from you. So you must have sold those ten policies." Mahesh kept mum. The Branch Manager asked again, "What happened, Mahesh?" To this, Mahesh replied sorrowfully, "No sir, I could sell only one policy." The Branch Manager was taken aback, and asked the reason. Mahesh replied that he used to send emails every day, but since he didn't get any positive response, he sent emails to more and more people and, in a similar manner, kept telephoning them as well. "Thus, I have worked hard for one month and finally was able to sell only a single policy."

The Branch Manager was surprised at the way Mahesh had been working. He was effort-oriented, but not result-oriented.

And then he asked Suresh, who replied, "Sir, neither could I send so many emails, nor could phone so many people. However, I have sold 10 policies." The Branch Manager was overjoyed and asked, "And how could you do this?"

Suresh replied that whatever happened with Mahesh had also happened with him. But he every time he heard a "No", he would ask the potential customers the reason why they did not want to take the policy. Thereafter, before making the next telephone call, he worked on his proposal and gave those examples which could possibly convince the customers that the policy was beneficial for them.

Suresh said that after making around 10 calls he was able to understand the manner in which he had to talk to the customers. He said, "During this one month I had the opportunity to meet around 30 persons and I could convince 10 of them to purchase. I concentrated on a few persons only and on their specific needs. I showed the insurance policies of our competitor companies to them and compared with our own policy. I could not talk to many persons, but exerted to find better options to satisfy their needs. Perhaps it is due to this that I was able to achieve my target."

The Branch Manager was very happy with the modus operandi of Suresh. He promoted Suresh and appointed him as the Team Leader.

What do we learn from this story? We learn that it is good to try, but you are not rewarded merely for your efforts; but for achieving results. So if you wish to achieve something in life, do not remain effort oriented, but rather become result oriented.

> **Arise! Awake! And wait not till the goal is reached.**
>
> **SWAMI VIVEKANAND**

The success of a result oriented approach depends on just three things:-
1. Your iron will to achieve the goal
2. Ability to look for alternatives
3. Positive thinking

We shall briefly discuss them .This shall help in making our life result oriented.

Your Iron Will to Achieve the Goal

To achieve any goal, it is extremely necessary to have an iron will.

If you consider just your efforts as your success, it means that the goal chosen is not very important in your life. In such a situation, you won't have an iron will. The goal should be such that it makes you constantly think, "If I have to do, I *have* to do." No other thought will do. If you have such a thought in your mind, there will be no excuses.

Ability to Look for Alternatives

The ability to look for alternatives is a great skill. Some people lose heart if they are unable to succeed with one approach. However, some persons do not lose heart till they have used all the available alternatives. Just think about the number of alternatives our martyrs searched for, in order to gain India's independence. They kept on meeting failures, and kept on looking for different alternatives. But they never lost hope.

Positive Thinking

It is vitally important to have positive thinking to achieve any result. We can move towards trying to achieve a new alternative only when we are optimistic about it. If we taste failure on the first attempt, and believe that we won't succeed after that, then we will never look for alternatives.

It is only when we get ourselves out of the dark alley of hopelessness, that we are able to look for newer alternatives to achieve the goal. And then, one of those alternatives will surely take us to our goal.

9

The Key to a Successful Plan Is Its Implementation

A good plan implemented today is better than a perfect plan implemented tomorrow

GEORGE PATTON

Any work starts with the making of a plan, but if the plan is not executed or implemented, it is of no use. In the chapter of Practical Plans, we tried to understand about making a good plan. In this chapter we shall throw light on its implementation.

There is a Sanskrit shloka, which is translated as:

> **The deeds of humans are successful only by hard work, and not by their wishing. No deer enters into the mouth of a sleeping lion.**

Even the king of the jungle, the lion, has to make an effort to catch its prey. For hours together, it has to sit for the ambush, and run faster than the deer. When it is so difficult for the lion, who is the king of the jungle, to get food, how can we think of getting success without hard work? There cannot be any alternative for success, and there is no alternative for hard work either.

One of the major reasons for non-execution of work is its postponement. There is a proverb, "Delay is denial," which means, "A delay in work is equivalent to a refusal to do it." A good execution depends upon the way you have put your heart into its planning, and the amount of will power you have for its implementation.

A plan remains a paper plan if there is absence of will power. But, those who have will power inside them, and are determined, can achieve success without any long-drawn plans. Let us learn from this story as to how important is will power for the execution of work:-

The Lost Opportunity

Once upon a time, there were two poor brothers who lived in the same house. Both were astrologers. The elder brother lived on the second floor while the younger one lived on the

The Key to a Successful Plan Is Its Implementation

ground floor. Their wives had different temperaments. The wife of the younger brother was a sharp-witted lady, always able to do her work in time, and ready to grab any opportunity for the betterment of the family. On the other hand, the wife of the elder brother was a lazy lady and took things for granted.

One day, an excited and happy elder brother approached his wife and told her that, by virtue of his astrological knowledge, he had a prophecy. He told her that if she got up at 2:00 am in the morning, and roasted some gram (Channa) seeds in a utensil, the gram seeds will turn into gold. The lazy lady heard this, but since it was a matter of getting up early in the morning, she ignored the whole issue.

On the other hand, this conversation was overheard by the younger brother's wife. The next morning she did as instructed by the elder brother and got the gold as was said.

The younger brother's wife went to the elder one and gifted her some of the gold.

The elder lady could do nothing but repent over her bad habit of laziness which let the opportunity escape.

> **A book bore the title "One hundred ways to catch mice."**
> **The book was eaten up by rats!**

Today, not only in the world of business, but also at home, family and society, those who work hard get rewarded with success and those who only make plans face poverty for years together.

Greatest Hurdle in the Way of Implementation — Excuses

Those who do not have a zeal for doing work, always make all sorts of excuses—for instance, "I am not well" (even if 100% healthy), "I do not feel like doing it," "I need someone to work with," "Let the winters pass," "I will do it in the new year," "My eye is twitching since this morning, it is better not to start work today," "Better not to work today at all," etc., etc. The excuses of worthless and lazy people never stop at any point.

I am a professor in a university. Every new semester, I am confronted with new and very interesting excuses from the students — especially on the day of the deadline for submission of their research project. Their excuses are often like "Sir, I am not able to comprehend the project," "My internet connection was not working," "I could not get any book on the subject," "There was a virus in my computer and the whole matter was wiped out," "My group member did not do any work," "Sir, the photocopy shop was closed,", and so on.

In fact, these are not excuses. These are indicators of lack of a strong will power. When I see the same students playing table tennis, cricket, and badminton or preparing for a cultural festival, I find that all their activities are on time — sometimes even before time. They may read the notice about the completion of a project or not, but they will always come to know of a party or celebration well in time. All this has a clear meaning — We always have the will for the work which we love to perform. But, to succeed in life, we often have to do many jobs which we do not like.

It is not surprising that, in the world of business, nobody wants excuses. You are expected to deliver results on time and if you make excuses regularly as a habit, eventually you will be fired from your job.

Today is the age of technology. You can't make an excuse saying, "I didn't know this," or "I could not inform," or "I could not get information." Your boss and colleagues will figure out immediately whether your reason is correct or just an excuse. So, work hard and don't make excuses.

> **I am not interested in excuses for delay.**
> **I am interested in getting things done.**
>
> **—JAWAHARLAL NEHRU**

We all know that we have to complete our work on time, but we do not do it, or are unable to do it. How can we solve this problem? I have some practical solutions for this:
1. Often, some resources are lacking and we keep on postponing the work. You must have heard many persons saying, "Just let me have this thing or facility

and I will work wonders." But, watch the lives of great people of the world. Abraham Lincoln did not have anything except an iron will, and he achieved what could be a dream for others. One of the first names among women entrepreneurs of India is Kiran Majumdar Shaw. She did not receive any help from anywhere, but didn't give up. She was able to set up the company Biocon Limited all by herself.

To start a work, do not wait for an auspicious day and time. By doing so, an opportunity which is at hand may simply slip away. That is why the learned and experienced persons say that the most auspicious day and time is *today* and *now*.

> **There is no ideal situation for initiating a work. Start with whatever is available right now. The position will keep on getting better.**

An Englishman was very impressed by the writings of *Munshi Premchand*. One day, he asked *Munshi Premchand*, "How do you manage to write so beautifully, with which pen and on what type of paper?" The Englishman expected a literary type of reply, but Munshi Premchand replied in a very humble manner, "I write with a pen which contains ink and on a paper on which nothing else has been written." Those who do extraordinary things do not need to show off.

1. **Develop the habit of doing things by yourself.** In the chapter on Time Management, we have stressed the fact that you can get things done by others so that your precious time can be saved. But some persons have the habit of not doing anything on their own. These so-called big people wait for their assistant, peon, or servants, for even their ordinary tasks, and this waiting is the cause of delay.

2. **Routine jobs** like photocopying, typing out an email, sending SMS, taking out a file, searching old mail, etc., can be done by anyone.

3. It is not necessary to always wait for assistants to do such jobs. If you are free, dispose them off immediately and move ahead towards your goal.

4. **Keep resources under your control.** There is a Sanskrit saying, "Knowledge written in a book and wealth gone into the hands of others—such knowledge and such wealth is of no use when needed." What we need to explain here is that, whenever starting a work, do not be lazy in collecting the necessary resources and keeping them available at hand, under your control. When your resources are with you, your work will keep on moving ahead. Do not sit idle by presuming that the resources will become available as and when the need comes up. Often, we trust others much more than required, and then presume that we can get the required things from them. But when the time comes, the person may not be available on the scene, or he or she may not be having the required item. This can jeopardize all your plans.

5. Keep in mind the fact **Burden of the head always falls on the feet.** This is a popular saying means that whatever burden you take will ultimately have to be performed by you anyway. This is important advice for those who tend to postpone work.

6. **Your work has to be done by you only,** and nobody else, whether you do it today or tomorrow. It is also said that today's work should never be left out for tomorrow. The more you keep on postponing your work, the more it keeps on accumulating. Ultimately, it adds up into a huge amount, which makes you either tense or anxious. So you start working day and night so as to finish that work. Working like this does not produce good quality output, nor does it produce a good effect.

Some persons postpone work and spend the time earmarked for doing it in loitering around. Realize that when you do this, the thoughts about the pending work keep on disturbing you. You meant to enjoy a stroll, but you know that you have to return for finishing that job. In such a situation, neither are you able to enjoy your stroll, nor able to do the work. Hence, it is better to dispose off your work in the first instance, and then spend time in enjoyment. Your enjoyment then will grow double-fold.

> **I hated each and every moment of my training, but said, "Do not lose, suffer right now, and then enjoy the rest of life being a Winner."**
>
> **MOHAMMAD ALI**

While executing any work, two words often come to mind of people — **Hard Work** and **Smart Work**. While choosing between the two, often Smart Work is chosen. However, these two concepts have their own importance. First, let us first understand the meaning of these terms.

Hard Work: Hard Work means doing work in a usual or traditional manner. Hard Work also means doing a lot of work, i.e., not wasting even a moment and focussing on its completion.

Smart Work: Smart Work means doing work using new and improved methods, so that time, money, and effort can be optimally utilized.

For achieving extraordinary success, we need to inculcate the ability to perform both Hard and Smart work. With the help of the diagram given below, let us see as to how we can do this. I have called it as **Hard Working with Smart Thinking**.

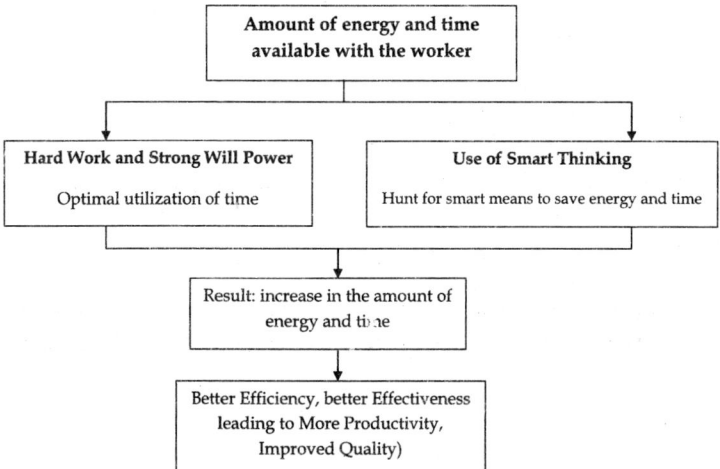

This diagram shows that hard work must be accompanied by smart thinking. Let us understand, by means of a story, as to how we can work with smart thinking:

Smart Work of Lord Ganesha

We all are aware that, among all the Hindu deities, the worship of Ganesh Ji is done first and foremost. There is a very interesting story behind this.

Once, all the gods had an argument as to who was the greatest among them who was to be worshipped first, before others. All of them were keen to prove themselves as the greatest. Not able to reach to a conclusion of the argument, they all went to Brahma Ji for a solution.

Brahma Ji told them that the god who makes a round of the earth and returns first, before others, will be considered as the greatest and he will be the one to be revered in the first place. On hearing this condition, all the gods immediately got into their respective vehicles and went off for orbiting around the earth. However, Ganesh Ji did not move from his place. He thought for a while and then went to his parents (Shiv-Parvati), requested them to sit together, and circled them. The other gods, returned one by one, after orbiting the earth. They found Ganesh Ji already present there. When Brahma Ji declared Ganesh Ji to have stood first in the competition and that he will be entitled to be worshipped first, all the gods were surprised. They said that Ganesh Ji never went out for the task and his vehicle, the rat, was extremely slow. If he had ridden on the rat, he could never have come first.

Hearing this, Brahma Ji said that Ganesh Ji, though his wit, has orbited around his mother (earth) and father (sky) and come first. So he was entitled to be worshipped first. Mother and father, together, are considered to be equivalent to the world. It is due to his wit and ability that Ganesh Ji has got the right to be worshipped first, before other gods.

> **If we do hard work with a smart method, we can not only change the course, but condition of our life as well.**

10
Knowledge Is the Foundation of Success

An interesting thing about knowledge is that the more we gain knowledge, the more we realize that we are less knowledgeable.

I will give you a formula of success — KC³ or KCCC, which means:

Knowledge X Communication X Confidence X Common Sense = Success

For success, you need to have all the above four capabilities. All these are a multiplication of one another. If the value of any one becomes zero, the result is zero. In this chapter we will discuss about the various aspects of knowledge such as: What is knowledge? What is the importance of knowledge? What are the different sources for different types of knowledge?

Knowledge is considered as power. There are many great personalities who have achieved success because of their vast knowledge. Ranging from scientists to poets and politicians to sportspersons, knowledge has always been the major contributor towards the success of everyone.

> **We must always try to learn and gain knowledge; pretending is useless, just like you cannot sell a cow that never gives milk, but remains decorated with bells around its neck**

What comes first — a dictionary or a word?

Answer..
Write your answer in the space given. I shall answer this question within this lesson only.

What Is Knowledge?

Most of us think that defining knowledge is very easy but this is not so easy. We think that whatever we know about our profession or business is our knowledge, but it is not true, because knowledge is much more than this. Intellectual power of human beings is divided into two parts — Theoretical Knowledge and Practical Knowledge. Theoretical knowledge is the knowledge found in books, learning from training programs, refresher courses, lectures etc. Practical knowledge is the knowledge gained from actually doing a job or practicing the theory, attending workshops and having hands on experience. We can learn it through "on the job training" also. With the help of following examples, the difference between theoretical knowledge and practical knowledge will be clearer:

- Your qualifications are basically your theoretical knowledge and your work experience is your practical knowledge.

- In technical and professional courses, the students are required to complete an internship of at least about 2-3 months. This is practical knowledge. But the exams they pass by reading books pertain to theoretical knowledge.

Before I proceed, I will answer the question I posed in the beginning of this lesson. What comes first, A Dictionary or a Word? I asked this question to establish a relationship between the theoretical and practical knowledge.

The correct answer is Word. If your answer is Dictionary, you are wrong. Words emerge during intellectual dialogues, discussions by poets, politicians and all others who wish to create new words during their conversations. These words are then adopted by the dictionaries leading to the dictionary becoming richer with every new edition. This example clearly shows that each and every part of theoretical knowledge comes from practice. In fact, whatever happens in practice, people learn from it and present it in the form of a book (theoretical knowledge).

Importance of Knowledge

No one can deny the importance of knowledge. But we cannot claim a particular type of knowledge is superior.

In some places theoretical knowledge is more important — for professors, writers, financial analysts, translators, etc., theoretical knowledge has a greater role to play. On the other hand, for sportspersons, soldiers, managers, etc., practical knowledge is required more. An intellectual person is always endowed with the treasure of knowledge and this treasure makes him or her employable anywhere and everywhere. They can easily earn their livelihood under all circumstances. They are respected everywhere. This has rightly been said in Sanskrit:

> **Winning a kingdom and acquiring knowledge can never be compared because a king is respected in his own kingdom only but an intellectual is respected throughout world.**

The entire world admits the power of intellectuals. We all know that this world is continuously advancing based on a strong intellect established by thousands of learned people such as Newton, Einstein, Aryabhata, Chanakya, etc. A knowledgeable person is never frustrated. His or her knowledge gives them power to get rid of all problems. Let us learn this with the help of a story about how even kings have to change their decision in front of intellectual people:

King Bhoj and the Weaver

King Bhoj was a successful emperor. People of his kingdom were great intellectuals.

One day, a learned person came to his court, and using his intellect, recited about the fame of the king in such a manner that the king was overjoyed and for every word uttered by the learned person, he gave away one lakh gold coins. The learned man was extremely happy. He praised the king even more, and requested King Bhoj to allow him to stay in his kingdom.

The king asked his courtiers to find a house in which the learned man could stay. The courtiers searched the entire kingdom, but could not find any suitable accommodation. They came back to the king and explained the situation. The king ordered them to find a person in the kingdom, who did not know Sanskrit language, and was unable to compose poetry in Sanskrit. He directed his men to evict that person from his house, and give that house to the learned man.

The courtiers made all endeavours to find out such a person, but everyone was well-read in the kingdom. After much searching, they found a weaver's house. The weaver was poor and used to earn his livelihood by weaving clothes. The courtiers made up their mind to catch hold of the weaver, and brought him to the king. The king told the weaver that he was not a learned person, nor could he compose poetry in Sanskrit and that was the reason of him being evicted from the kingdom.

To this, the weaver replied humbly in the form of a Sanskrit poem. The meaning of the poem was, "O king, I can compose poem. My ordinary poem is not so beautiful, but if I compose it with a joyful heart, then it comes out to be extremely beautiful. I weave cloth for my livelihood, and compose poem in ecstasy, and so goes on my life. Even then if you ask me to leave, I shall do so."

The king was amazed and happy as well on discovering the weaver's vast knowledge. He immediately directed the courtiers to escort the weaver to his house, and asked to accommodate the learned person in the royal palace till appropriate arrangements could be made.

This is the importance of knowledge.

> **I always believe in recruiting people who are smarter than me.**
>
> **N R NARAYANA MURTHY, FOUNDER—INFOSYS**

To be knowledgeable we need to increase our knowledge on daily basis or else we won't be able to face the challenges of this highly competitive world.

Many of us assume that we have sufficient knowledge required for our job or career and there is no need to learn more. I specifically ask a question here:

Do You Think Your Knowledge Is Enough?

We always learn from our elders that "Learning is the process which never ends," which means that even in your profession, you do not know all and that there is always more scope of learning. You ought to build a learning attitude. We need to accept that we do not know everything and can get better results by increasing the level of our knowledge and can become the best in our profession. Let's start practicing:

1. Do you think the syllabus of all subjects you have studied in your student life was able to cover 100% of the area it belonged to?
2. Do you think the books recommended by your teachers and institution/university were able to cover 100% of the subject for which they were written? (Please note, if a book matches the syllabus it does not mean that it contains 100% knowledge of that subject)
3. Do you think that you learned 100% of each topic discussed in the class?
4. Do you think that the exams you took covered 100% of the knowledge relating to that subject?
5. Do you think that you could fill the entire gap after you started working in any institution?

If the answer of any of the above questions is "No", then you need to learn more.

How do we gain knowledge?

You need to be very polite and accept yourself to be open-minded before you begin to learn something. If you are of the opinion that you need not learn anything, you will cease to grow any more. I would like to share a story about the learning attitude.

Story of Swami Vivekananda

The story is set in the time when Swami Vivekananda was searching for a Guru. Different people suggested different saints. He would approach every saint but was never satisfied. During his exhaustive search someone recommended Swami Ramkrishan Paramhans. Swami Vivekanand had heard a lot about him and he considered himself to be very fortunate to meet Swami Ramkrishan Paramhans. He also was aware that Swami Paramhans had no disciples and he would not easily accept someone as his student. This also increased the curiosity of Swami Vivekanand and now he was more than eager to meet Paramhans.

Finally one day Swami Vivekanand went to Swami Ramkrishan Paramhans, and knocked at his door. On being asked by Swami Ramkrishan— Paramhans "Who is this?" Vivekanand Ji replied, "That is what I have come to know—Who am I?" Swami Ramkrishan Paramhans happily accepted Vivekanand as his disciple.

> A true disciple is the one who surrenders himself or herself to learn.

Do you have such attitude for learning? Remember the example of Eklavya who learned with the help of only a statue of his guru, Guru Dronacharya! Do you think the statue of guru Dronacharya taught him anything? No! It was the learning attitude of Eklavya which made him master the skill of archery.

I have come across people who would sit for more than 10-12 hours a day and utilize every single minute of their time to learn something new, leading to growth in knowledge. Gaining knowledge or learning is not only limited to your student life. Even if you are a working professional, there is always a scope for learning. Nowadays thousands of workshops, crash courses, short-term courses, online courses, and management development programmes are organized by independent institutions, universities, and autonomous bodies. You can attend them to enhance your knowledge. I have given some important categories of knowledge and the sources from where you can learn:

Level of Importance	Type of Knowledge	Source
Most Important	The Core knowledge as well as additional knowledge related to your profession or business, which is the result of innovations and new technologies. If you grasp it, you can be an expert of the contemporary techniques in your field. This will not only help you in your day to day work but also increase the chances of your career growth.	This knowledge is acquired from the advanced courses, workshops, etc. In the field of Management IIMs and other top B-Schools and in the field Technology, IITs are some of the major institutions imparting such knowledge. Apart from them, some other private and government institutions also offer contemporary short term courses.
Very Important	The knowledge which was an integral part of your degree or diploma course, but due to some reason you skipped it. Now you can read some books to strengthen that missed theoretical knowledge.	Reference books are the best source of this category of knowledge. The names of best reference books can be obtained from your college teachers or from online book stores or similar sources.

Level of Importance	Type of Knowledge	Source
Important	General Knowledge (G.K.) is the knowledge which is important in our personal and professional life. G.K. is not considered very important by many of us but it gives a very good impression about the speaker during many formal and informal discussions.	Examples: What is the product we are going to buy? Which company has produced it? Which is the best brand? What is happening on the political front? Which T.V. show is attracting maximum TRP? Something about new books, new authors, new film stars, etc. For G.K., you can tune into some news channels for 20–30 minutes a day or read newspapers and magazines regularly. Whenever you find something new while discussing with people, try to probe more to know the details.

I believe that the above activities will not only motivate you to increase your knowledge but also help you in finding numerous ways to enhance the same.

> **Anyone who stops learning is old, whether at twenty or eighty. Anyone who keeps learning stays young. The greatest thing in life is to keep your mind young.**
>
> **HENRY FORD**

11
Communication — Make the Best of It

It is so true that "many people do not talk sense and many do not speak even when required to do so."

The power of speaking is the greatest boon given to man by God. However, there is a big difference between the **power to speak** and the **art of speaking**. We call the art of speaking *communication skill* or the *art of conversation*. Many people are well-versed in this art and they win the hearts of the others. They never clash with anyone, and are never entangled in any type of controversy. In fact, being aware of what is to be said, where, to whom, when, why, and how is a great art. The famous Urdu poet **Waseem Barelvi** has aptly said:

> *Kaun si baat, kahan, kaise kahi jati hai*
> *Yeh saleeka ho toh har baat suni jaati hai*

(What should we say? Where? and How? If we have this skill, we will always be heard)

On several occasions, keeping quiet is an intelligent option and superfluous talking becomes unwanted and inappropriate. There is a Sanskrit saying: *Vaktaro dardush yatra, tatra maunam hi shobhanam* which means it is better to be silent in a situation where frogs are croaking.

Many people make mistakes in communication and others get annoyed with them. Let us now see how the hero of this story, Bholuram, had to suffer due to the wrong use of words in his speech:

The Blunder of Bholuram

In a village, there lived an unemployed man by the name of Bholuram. He was extremely poor. One day, his wife asked him to go to town and get a job. As Bholuram was about to leave, his wife handed him a packet of rice and told him to get the rice cooked in any house on the way whenever he felt hungry. Bholuram nodded and started his journey, carrying the rice with him. While crossing a village, he started feeling hungry. Looking around for a house, he saw one at some distance and he knocked at the door. An old lady appeared and asked the purpose of his coming. Bholuram replied that he had travelled from a faraway village and he was very hungry. He had some rice with him. If the rice could be cooked, he could satisfy his hunger. The old lady liked the simplicity of Bholuram. She said that she had some milk from her buffalo, and if the rice was given to her, she could prepare "kheer" for Bholuram.

The old lady took Bholuram inside her house, added the milk to the rice and put it on the fire for boiling, in the kitchen. Next to the kitchen, the buffalo was tied with a rope. Bholuram started gazing at the buffalo, and then asked, "Mai, your buffalo is quite large, but the door of your house is very small. How did you manage to get it inside?" The old lady, looking lovingly at her buffalo, replied, "You are right, son, but when I had brought it, it was an infant, and was very small, hence I was able to get her inside, through this small door. I have fed it well and now it is big in size." Bholuram's mind did not rest by this reply, because he was an epitome of simplicity. He instantly reacted, "But, Mai, there is a problem." The old lady asked, "What is it?" Bholuram said, "When your buffalo dies, how will you get it out?"

On hearing this, the old lady was shocked. She was extremely angry, and screamed, "You scoundrel, how can you even imagine the death of my beloved buffalo, from whose milk this kheer is being prepared, which you were about to consume? Take your rice and get out of here!" She poured the half-cooked kheer into the packet in which Bholuram had carried the rice, and threw him out of her house. When he came out with the packet, milk trickling out of it, someone asked, "What is this thing trickling?" To this, the old woman screamed from inside, "It is the scoundrel's manner of talking which is trickling."

> **We should remain quiet rather than gossiping unnecessarily, or we should talk something as a better than silence.**

Lessons from the Story

- While talking to a person just for the sake of interaction, talk only positive things and not negative about anybody. Do not indulge in a controversial discussion.

- Before saying anything, think twice whether it is likely to hurt the other person.
- Conversation made even for simply chatting is also very significant. If proper care is not exercised during the conversation, it can be a cause of trouble for you.

The greatest challenge before us today is how to use this art of conversation so that we may receive the maximum benefit from it in our business and social life. In today's world, communication has such a lot of power that many people are using their communication ability as professionals to run their enterprise. Knowledge of language and its proper use helps us to reach a leadership position in our respective work areas.

The world of communication is extremely vast. Its complicated structure can be understood with the help of following diagram:

When you talk to a person for official or personal purpose through a specific, effective medium, through carefully chosen words, and with a specific formal purpose, it is called *Formal Communication*. When we communicate for a personal purpose, whether socially or at the workplace, it is called *Informal Communication*. This can be understood with the help of the following matrix:

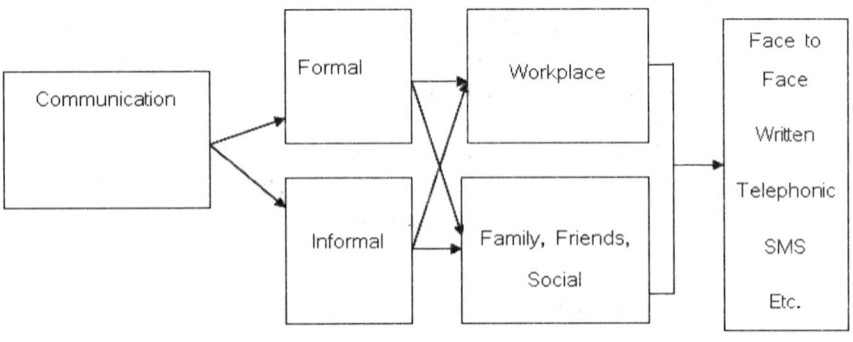

	Workplace	Family, Friends, Social
Formal	Office meetings; presentations; meeting with client or telephonic Discussion; any written or oral official conversation with seniors, juniors, or peers in office.	Respect of elders or eminent social persons in family or social gathering; formal invitation to friends, relatives, and nearby people on any auspicious occasion; discussion with any of the above people on some formal matter.
Informal	Gossiping with peers; discussion during birthday celebrations, lunch breaks, tea breaks; any written or oral communication with boss, juniors, or peers regarding personal life.	Gossiping with family members, friends, neighbours; chatting done for the purpose of passing time and without specific objective; jokes and fun with family and friends on any occasion.

> **Some persons take informal communication very casually, though it acts as the foundation for a long term relationship.**

The definition and description of formal and informal communication is extremely extensive, and is outside the scope of this book. I have only tried to explain their meaning through an illustration.

Till now we have discussed some basic facts about the art of conversation. Now, we shall try to understand the complexities involved in the medium of communication. At times, you must have seen that some persons talk a lot without committing mistakes, while others, who are less vocal, speak meaningless words on the few occasions when they open their mouths. Why does this happen? Let us discuss this issue.

The art of conversation cannot be learnt in a single day; it takes a long time. Before speaking anything, we must keep in mind the following points:

1. What relation do we have with the person with whom we are talking? We are junior to our boss. Likewise, we are bosses in front of our juniors. We have to choose words, body language, and mannerisms accordingly.

2. How significant is our role in the situation where we are placed? It has to be checked whether we keep on talking without any legitimate right, which may eventually lead to an insult.

3. What are the end results of our talking or keeping quiet? If you cannot take a decision quickly, defer that decision and do not say anything at all. In such matters, always think and then express your opinion.

4. Written and public (oral) communication is an extremely serious subject. In written communication, anything communicated from your side acts as a proof. So, never give anything in writing which may land you into trouble in the future. I always want my students to know that:

You have to pay for your words and actions, if not today, then definitely tomorrow.

While involved in public speaking, be very vigilant, as often people blurt out things out of enthusiasm which can pose problems and you may be unable to give an explanation later. In the bargain, some people may get annoyed with you. I, being a lecturer and a poet, have an experience of speaking on almost 1,000 occasions, and have learnt that addressing any type of audience involves a huge amount of responsibility. The slightest mistake committed can become a cause for trouble and awkwardness for the speaker.

12

Becoming an Expert in Business Communication

The most *important* thing *in communication* is to hear what isn't being *said.*

PETER F. DRUCKER

The maximum need for expertise in communication occurs in interviews, group discussions, public speaking, etc. In this chapter you will see how you can maximize your communication skills.

Communication Skills for Interview

In the world of business today, for getting a job, interview is considered to be the most important method. It is often observed that the applicant takes the interview rather too seriously, or too lightly.

Both these approaches prove to be harmful to the candidate. As this chapter deals with the subject of communication, we shall limit our discussion to the importance of communication in an interview.

In an interview, not only the choice of words, but *body language* also plays a very important role. A candidate, while facing the interview, should make the following preparations in advance:

1. **Your description in brief and in detail:** In almost every interview you are asked about this. In the process, try not to stress more on one particular issue. Mention briefly about family, your qualifications, with a mention about your special achievements (your projects, awards, etc.). However, you can always talk more on a subject which is directly relevant in getting the job.

2. **Frequently asked questions:** For instance, How are you suited for this particular job? What are your main plus points which can prove to be useful for the company? What have you learnt from your work experience? Why do you want to leave your old company? Where do you see yourself five or ten years

from now? If selected, can you join immediately? How will you manage to live here? How much salary do you expect?

If you enter the interview room after making these preparations, then you are sure to have an effective communication.

3. **Replying in the right manner:** Listen to every question attentively. While replying to questions, be precise, do not divert from the point, and do not linger on a single issue. While replying to the questions of the interview panel, maintain eye contact. Never argue on the subject matter of a question. Also, do not show off your knowledge. Nevertheless, if you feel that something worth mentioning can prove to be beneficial for you, then you can mention it with appropriate humility.

4. **Body Language:** In an interview, body language plays an extremely important role. In the parlance of communication, we call it as "Non-Verbal Communication", which means *talking without words*. In an interview, your attitude should neither be to remain extremely sad, not extremely happy and carefree. A calm expression on the face and a slight smile on the lips is an essential body language for the interview. Your manner of entering the interview room, mannerism in sitting down and standing up, etc., should all reflect simplicity as well as respect for the interviewers. Any show of arrogance can affect your chance of getting selected.

Importance of Communication in Group Discussion

In managerial and technical education, group discussion is of vital importance for the students. For getting admission to an MBA course, and also for getting selected in business organizations, group discussion is an important tool. For

participating in a group discussion, you must bear in mind the following points:
1. Do not keep talking all by yourself. *Give others also a chance to speak.*
2. Speak in a balanced manner. Also, *do not keep absolutely silent.* Contribute your share in making the discussion reach a culmination point.
3. When the discussion starts diverting from its path, *put it back on the right track.* By doing so, you will get additional points.
4. Some persons believe that irrelevant matters, if put forth in a *loud manner,* is correct in a group discussion. However, this displays their lack of knowledge. Talking loudly may prove to be negative for you.
5. Never turn a group discussion into an *argument.*
6. Whenever countering a participant's point, never attempt to use *defamatory or insulting words.* Do not put the other person down; rather explain the significance of your point in a logical manner.
7. Always be *result-oriented,* and try to make a conclusion from the ongoing discussion.
8. Use *polite and courteous* words. Your language reflects your knowledge. Your words reveal as to what type of a person you are. This will give immense benefits in the long run.

Importance of Communication in Public Speaking

"Public Speaking" is said to be the most difficult way of conversation. You must have witnessed or heard of *stage fear* being displayed in many persons. You must also have seen people with trembling legs while standing on the stage. Some persons can talk well in meetings, group discussions, and interviews. But, when asked for public speaking, the moment they ascend the platform, their voice and legs both start trembling. They tend to forget whatever statements they have to make, cannot use appropriate words, and ultimately become a medium for amusement of others. In communication, public speaking has never been considered necessary for every person. Nevertheless, in this age, this quality can add to your personality in a big way.

Public speaking is not related directly to the number of persons in the audience. *A process where you have to come on stage and face an audience in order to communicate your ideas can be called public speaking.* In order to address people from the stage, and address them in an effective manner, you have to bear the following points in mind:

1. *Before giving a speech*

a. Never agree to give a speech, or even try for it, which is outside the scope of your knowledge.
b. Know fully well about the subject of your speech, number of listeners, chief guest, special invitees, other speakers, and the organizers of the programme.
c. You also need to know some things about the audience, e.g., the language in which they would prefer to listen to your speech, the region to which they belong, the level of their education, etc.

2. *During the programme*

a. While sitting and waiting for your turn to deliver the speech, pay attention to the subject matter of the programme, remarks by the anchor, and the speeches of other speakers. This will provide not only a good quality of information for your own speech, but also increase your own confidence. You can jot down the important points as well.

b. While other speakers are giving their speech, do not waste your time in gossiping outside the auditorium. It is possible that whatever you wish to say may be said by an earlier speaker, and your speech may lose its effect.

c. While listening to the other speakers, avoid using your mobile phone, or reading a magazine, or chatting with somebody. This amounts to an insult to the speaker who is speaking at that moment.

3. *During your own speech*

a. Use the normal rules of communication, viz., sweetness of language, avoidance of defamatory words against anyone, not drifting away from the main subject, etc.

b. Maintain a constant eye contact with the audience and other speakers.

c. Keep a special consideration for time limit. Do not pose problems for the organizers by taking extra time over allotted one. Many times, we forget the time available due to the momentum of speech, as we have much to talk about. However, it is better to avoid talking more, and talk important matters in least time, thus displaying your expertise.

d. For time management, we can also use our wrist watch or mobile phone.

e. Keep a control over your emotions, and do not claim the good or bad regarding anything without facts.

f. Avoid criticism, but do not miss to talk with readily available facts which are important for the subject.

g. Always praise and encourage those speakers who have mentioned good points.

4. After the speech

After delivering your speech, you tend to become stress-free. In such a situation, you must listen to the other speakers, which is extremely important. Some persons, after delivering their speech, tend to slip away from the place. However, this does not come in the category of decency. Just ponder over it, if all speakers do this, the last speaker will lose almost all enthusiasm. Stay till the end of the programme, and then thank the organizers and congratulate them for the success of the event.

Communication Skill for Corporate Presentations

In today's scenario, in the world of industry and in business schools and universities, computerized presentation in the form of Power Point and Digital Board are quite common. These methods help you in giving a good presentation. They also help the audience to understand the subject matter easily. However, inability to utilize these tools in a proper manner often turns your presentation ineffective.

To make an effective Power Point presentation, three points should be kept in mind:
1. Subject matter of the presentation.
2. Presentability of the subject matter.
3. Communication skills while making the presentation.

In a presentation, it is difficult to say as to which of the above is more important. Without the subject matter, nothing can be presented, but whenever there is a mention of Power Point presentation, the element of presentability is also very important, i.e., design of the slides, number of words on a single slide, size of words, colour, use of pictures and audio-visuals, etc.

Regarding the subject matter, the following things must be borne in mind:

1. While preparing a presentation, we must make the maximum use of the different sources of information, e.g., the internet, books, magazines and periodicals, etc. Never prepare the presentation based on a single source.

2. While borrowing material from the internet, always take care that you are borrowing it from a reliable website. These days there are a number of websites and blogs on which people just discuss and pass their spare time and this type of information is not trustworthy.

3. The presentation should be centred on the main subject matter. You should give a summary of the contents in the very beginning, so that the audience get an idea of what they are going to listen in the coming moments.

4. Use data charts, wherever possible, as it makes the presentation more effective. The data can be presented in the form of table, graph or bar or pie chart, and not just in the form of a paragraph.

5. Along with the main points, pictures, and data, the footnotes of slides must contain references. It is difficult to rely on information which does not carry a reference.

6. The presentation should be limited on the basis of time available.

In order to make the presentation more attractive in terms of its presentability, the following points are worth considering:

In one Power Point slide, do not write more than 50 words. Write them point-wise, and not in a paragraph style, otherwise it will be of no use to the audience. You can grasp these two things by the following illustration:

(A)

The significance of retail business in India and foreign investment
In India, retail business occupies a very important place as it gives employment to 1 crore 20 lakh persons. Its contribution to the GDP is 14-15%, and its gross size is approx. US $ 450 crores. Presently, foreign investment has been allowed in retail business. The present level of foreign investment is 100% in Wholesale Cash and Carry, 100% in Single Brand, and 51% in Multi Brand. Many persons will be affected by foreign investment; the ones to get affected mainly will be farmers and small-time businessmen. The government has formed certain rules for this. Foreign investment in retail business shall not be applicable to towns having a population less than 10 lakhs.

(B-1)

The significance of retail business in India
1. Retail business provides employment to approximately 1 crore 20 lakh people
2. It has a contribution of 15% to the GDP.
3. In India, its total size is approximately US $ 450 crores.

(B-2)

Foreign investment in retail business
1. The level of foreign investment in retail business in India:
• 100% in wholesale Cash & Carry
• 100% in Single Brand
• 51% in Multi Brand
2. Mainly farmers and small businessmen will be affected from foreign investment.
3. Foreign investment in retail business will not be applicable in towns having a population of less than 10 lakhs.

1. Look carefully at the three slide designs. Design A appears to be a page from any book. It contains two subjects in a single slide. This slide contains many words and it has been constructed like a paragraph, which will make the audience to read it with difficulty. Underlined lines appear to be extremely ordinary, which the speaker can speak all by himself or herself, and it was not necessary to write them on the slide. Now, look carefully at slide designs B-1 and B-2. In it, the requisite subject matter has been mentioned, and all unnecessary material has been removed. Here, the words are bigger in size and, the subject matter is in a point-wise style, both the slides are clear in expression. They have 41 and 66 words respectively. In slide B-2, the first point also carries sub-points, so that the audience may grasp it immediately.

2. Always use pictures in the slides so that they look attractive. For instance, if your presentation is regarding Retail Business, you can use the picture of a mall or a retail shop. In the same manner, a presentation on various topics can be made to look better by use of related pictures. Choice of pictures can be made on the basis of the main subject, as well as on the basis of the subject matter of the particular slide.

3. Presentation can be made to look better through the use of different colours for different letters, sizes and shapes, etc. The presentation can be made easy-to- understand by using a separate colour for each heading, separate colour for ordinary sentences, and a unique colour for displaying important information.

4. The role of data is extremely important in any presentation. Specific data can be displayed in a separate colour in any line of the paragraph. However, if it is a group of data pertaining to a specific subject,

then it is desirable to display through the medium of a table.

In the actual presentation, we must follow the rules of Public Speaking. Also, the following points are worth considering:
1. While doing a Power Point presentation, some presenters making the mistake of reading the material given in the slide only. This is the worst kind of presentation.
2. Power Point slides are for reference only, and not for "reading out a letter". They are meant to assist you and the audience, and you can glance at them only occasionally. You can use the slide to take the reference of the data, or for a description of the chart. But reading out the whole information given in the slide is absolutely *not* recommended.
3. While addressing the audience, do not look continuously at the Power Point. Your main task is to address the audience. To make this easier, you can use the display at two places. One display can be in the laptop in front of you, and the other behind you, through the LCD projector, for the audience.

Praising in an Appropriate Manner

Everybody has their own style of giving praise. Some praise openly, while others merely say, "Very good" or "Bravo". Whenever you praise someone, praise them sincerely. Otherwise, the praised person might perceive it as a mere formality. Recall the person's qualities, activities, and achievements and praise them. If you want to praise any speaker, you can do so by quoting a piece of the subject matter of their speech, in the form of a sentence or a part of a sentence or an example they have given, so that the person realizes that you have actually heard the speech. If you wish to praise someone's dress, you can do so by admiring the colour of the shirt, trousers, or suit. When we praise someone, it should not be in an ordinary, routine manner but rather by pinpointing at his or her special quality. Then this praise turns out to be more effective, and it does not look merely a formality.

We must not praise too much. Often, we are very impressed by characteristics such as the personality, qualities of an individual, etc. However if we start praising a person profusely, we might do it with all sincerity, not with any sarcastic intention, but others often perceive it as an act of unnecessary flattery. Therefore it is advisable not to go overboard with the praise.

13

Not Letting Your Self-Confidence to Be Shaken

The first pre-requisite for performing a great deed is self-confidence.

SAMUEL JOHNSON

Self-confidence is that power within a person which not only transforms their personality into an optimistic one, but also makes them strong to face the difficulties that would be there in the way of success.

Self-confidence and *confidence* are two different things. You have confidence in someone else, but self-confidence is in your own self, that is, the confidence you have on yourself. Self-confidence is the first thing which a person wants to see in himself or herself. Also, it is said, "First you have confidence in yourself, and then the world shall have confidence in you."

Before reading further, please answer the following question:

In 1983, when the Indian cricket team was playing against West Indies in the World Cup, what would the captain of the team, Kapil Dev, be thinking:

1. *We cannot win* as West Indies has won the World Cup twice, and they shall *defeat us* and become World Cup winner for the third time.

2. *We may be able to win*, but it is an extremely difficult. I think *we cannot win*.

3. From our side, we can do the best, but there are *least chances* of winning.

4. *Although it is extremely difficult to win*, still we shall perform our best.

5. *We can definitely win*, if we work very hard. When we were able to defeat England and many other countries in the World Cup and were able to reach the final, we have the capacity to win the finals as well.

6. *We have already won.* This one is a practice match for the next World Cup.

Think it over and then answer!

I know that many people will choose Serial nos. 4 or 5, because these two are the indicators of self-confidence. Some may also choose 6, but this displays an *over self-confidence*. Let us see, which one of the 6 points is the most appropriate to define self-confidence:

1. No self-confidence
2. Very low self-confidence
3. Low self-confidence
4. Medium level of self-confidence
5. High level of self-confidence
6. Too much self-confidence

According to you, what is the source of self-confidence?

There are many sources of self-confidence. The most important one is *knowledge*. Merely having knowledge is not a guarantee of the fact that you have a very high level of self-confidence. Let us understand how this happens

Acquiring Knowledge to Boost Self-Confidence

Let us understand this with the help of an example. Suppose you are sitting in a seminar hall. All of a sudden, the anchor announces your name and asks you to put forth some ideas on the subject of advertising. Unfortunately, you do not know anything about advertising. What will be the level of your self-confidence?

Let us take one more example which displays the significance of knowledge for the sake of self-confidence: Remember your student days. What was the level of your self-confidence when the teacher asked questions in the class? You will say that it all depends on the question asked. You are absolutely right. Against the reply of a student, I have allotted a certain percentage for a typical reply. Try to understand this example:

	Question	Level of self-confidence
1.	What is the name of the Prime Minister of India?	95%
2.	Who is the founder of Face book?	50%
3.	Who was the first lady chief minister of an Indian state?	5%

Look closely at the questions and the level of self-confidence rated against these. This is an illustration. The first question is quite easy, and there are good chances that you will have its answer. Hence, there are chances that your self-confidence in it is 95% or more. If the teacher asks this question, you will immediately raise your hand for making a reply.

The second question looks a bit difficult. You may recall its answer, but you will not raise your hand as your level of self-confidence in regard to this question is only 50%. However, if your teacher asks you to try to answer this question, you will answer it, although with hesitation.

In the third situation, the question is quite difficult. One or two names do strike your mind, but you know well that these names may not be the correct answers. Your level of self-confidence is just 5%. In such a situation, you will neither raise your hand not will you answer the question even if the teacher asks, as you have a negligible confidence in your answer.

I hope that by now you have understood the significance of knowledge. A detailed description of knowledge has already been discussed in one of the previous chapters.

> **Knowledge invokes a feeling of capability inside you, and this feeling transforms into your self-confidence.**

Discovering Your Potential

The other source of self-confidence is knowledge about your capabilities. But this is not so easy. For this, we have to know our self. Often, a person can very easily tell the capabilities of someone else, but knows very little about himself or herself. It is also true that when you discover your own powers, your self- confidence increases manifold. Let us understand this by way of the story of Hanuman Ji, as to how your self-confidence is the discovery of your own powers:

Power Realization by Hanuman Ji

Who is not aware of the courage of Hanuman Ji? However, once upon a time the self-confidence of Hanuman Ji had been dormant. It was activated by the great bear Jambwant, the senior warrior of the army of Sugreev. The monkey group, which consisted of the senior monkeys Angad, Nal, Neel, Hanuman, etc., while going southward in search of Mother Sita came to know that Ravan had taken Sita Ji to Lanka, which was situated near the seashore. Then, while everyone was discussing about their individual strength for crossing the sea, Hanuman Ji was standing quietly.

Everyone was surprised to see that Hanuman Ji was standing quietly. Then, Jambwant said to him, "O brave Hanuman, it is you alone who can cross this vast sea, and can come back, too." But, Hanuman Ji was all confused at that time and kept standing. He was unable to see his hidden powers. Jambwant told him that, since childhood, he was powerful. During his childhood he had greatly disturbed the rishis and munis, and they had laid a curse on him that he shall forget about all his powers, till someone reminded him about them.

Jambwant, reminding Hanuman Ji of his powers, said, "O brave Bajrangbali, you are the same one who had playfully gulped the Sun inside your mouth. Then, nobody could stop you, and Indra had no option but to shoot off his Vajra. You are the form of Shiv, the son of Pawan Dev, and the ultimate devotee of Lord Ram.

On listening about his powers from Jambwant, Hanuman Ji could immediately recall about his hidden powers. As soon as he recalled his powers, his self-confidence shot up. He roared "Jai Shree Ram", and set out in search of Mata Sita.

> **You have to awaken your powers by yourself, because the people of this age are very busy. You cannot wait for a Jambwant to come.**

There is a magnificent way to awaken your powers— *listing out your achievements.* For instance, we said in the World Cup final match incident that "Kapil Dev must have thought that when we have reached up to this point after defeating big teams like England. . . ." etc. This is called as recalling your own achievements. To awaken your powers, make a list of even your smallest achievement. You will realize that you have ample capacity, and you that you can do equally well what is being done by today's successful orators, professionals, managers, industrialists, and officers.

Compare Yourself with Great People Who Started Out as Ordinary People

When you start comparing yourself with persons who were extremely ordinary during their childhood, or even worse than the situation in which you are at present, then your self-confidence increases. You start thinking, "when these people can become successful, why not me?" There are plenty of such examples.

N. R. Narayanamurthy, one of the founders of one of the biggest Indian software companies, Infosys, borrowed a mere Rs. 10,000 from his wife, Sudha, and started Infosys. However, the self-confidence he had in him was immeasurable. As a result of this, his total wealth in 2015 was $ 1.8 billion.

Can an attendant at a petrol pump establish India's biggest private enterprise? Yes. If there is self-confidence like Dhirubhai Ambani, then everybody can.

Comedy king Raju Srivastava, started his career as a mimic of Amitabh Bachchan. But, it was his self-confidence which made him popular among the masses and made him a leader of stand-up comedy.

Many of the bestsellers of the world have been rejected by not one, but many publisher. However, their authors did not lose heart and kept trying for getting their work published, because they had confidence on their creation. It was this confidence which made their books a "bestseller". The best example of this is the Harry Potter series authored by J. K. Rowling. The first book of this series was rejected by 12 publishers!

In fact, **every great personality has humble beginnings. It is through, their hard work which makes him a great person.** Every person is born with some quality or the other. You need to simply recognize those qualities, make your strength, and persist and practice on them. You will gain self-confidence and your aim will be achieved automatically.

A politician visited a village and with a lot of pride he asked a simple farmer, "Listen, has any great man taken birth in your village?"

The farmer replied with utter innocence, "No sir, only children take birth here."

14

Common Sense — the Most Useful Element

Common sense is knowledge that we do not realize when it is present, but when it is missing, we can easily notice it.

Common sense, i.e., normal intelligence, is considered to be a very useful element. But, how do we define common sense?

Common Sense is that minimum intelligence which is expected to be possessed by every individual.

In other words, common sense is that amount of basic intelligence which is expected to be found in every person. But, it is often said "Common sense is very uncommon", i.e., even the minimal amount of intelligence is lacking in many individuals. In such a situation, the bid to understand the meaning of common sense becomes all the more necessary.

Common sense is not taught, but it develops over time in an individual. You cannot learn common sense from books, nor can anyone train you in it. In fact, it originates from your quick thinking and the amount of knowledge you have. With the help of a small illustration, let us look how common sense is important in day-to-day life:

Laugh While You Learn

A manager, before proceeding on a tour abroad for a fortnight, instructed his assistant to receive all the postal mail in his absence, and mark each letter with date on which it was received. The assistant said, "Sir, please do not worry. I will write on every letter the date of its receipt."

After 15 days, the manager came back from his overseas trip, and asked the assistant, "Bring the letters received in my absence. Did you note when each letter was received?" The assistant replied, "Yes, sir, I have noted on all the letters." He brought the letters to the manager. On seeing them, the manager got very angry and screamed at the assistant. Can you imagine what the assistant had written on those letters?

The assistant had written on each letter, "Received today"!

This is called a lack of common sense. The Assistant could not comprehend what the manager wanted him to write, and for what purpose. This is why it is said that *Common sense is very uncommon.*

Why, When and Where is Common Sense Really Needed?

Common sense is not a permanent thing. It is dynamic and keeps on changing with **time, circumstances, and situation.**

You must always bear in mind as to what type of intelligence is required in a particular situation. For instance, in a condolence meeting, we do not go with gaudy clothes, and keep quiet. These are some of the small things which do not need any specific training, but these are expected from you.

An illustration of lack of common sense is given below:

A young man was being interviewed for the post of typist. As he entered in the interview room, he was asked by one of the interviewers, "What is your speed?"

The interviewee questioned, "Of what, Sir?"

The interviewer said "You can leave. Gentleman, we are not asking about your speed of running or driving; we are just interested in your typing speed."

We have to strengthen our common sense for all types of circumstances. To understand this in depth, some examples of common sense are given:

1. Listening attentively to the boss, not praising the juniors excessively, and keeping good terms with the peers is common sense.
2. Not taking a mobile phone inside an examination hall. Wearing formal clothes in a conference or a presentation, avoiding political and office discussions in a personal programme. These are all included in common sense.

3. While facing an interview board, never arguing with a board member, not making adverse comments about the previous employer, and giving proper salutation to all the members while answering a question — this all is common sense.
4. In an interview, you elaborate on your successes or your strengths and not on your failures or weaknesses. This is common sense.
5. If, while giving a PowerPoint presentation, a particular slide has a wrong word, then you explain the slide quickly, and carry on smoothly — this is common sense.
6. You are an insurance agent. You client has agreed to buy a policy from you and asked you to come home and collect the cheque. When you reach the client, you find that the client's son has suddenly fallen ill. You tell the client to look after the son, and return back without mentioning anything about the cheque — this is common sense.

Common sense is needed most when a task is not accomplished as per your plans, and a new circumstance has appeared. Or, when you face a situation which is new to you. For instance, in the corporate world, men often shake hands, but with ladies common sense says that only when the lady extends her hand for a handshake, then only should a gentleman return the handshake.

Let us look at a story to understand how common sense helps us in adverse circumstances:

Laugh While You Learn

Once, Shani Dev and Lakshmi Ji started arguing as to who was better looking among the two. They approached Brahma Ji and asked him. Brahma Ji was very intelligent, and did not

Common Sense – the Most Useful Element

want to annoy either of them, so he replied, "Both of you are good-looking." Both understood the purpose behind the reply of Brahma Ji, and again asked, "No, please tell us as to who is better looking among us." To this, Brahma Ji pointed towards the earth and said, "Look down on the earth. There is a trader's shop over there. He is very intelligent. Go to him; he will certainly reply to your question."

So Shani Dev and Lakshmi Ji approached the trader. Seeing both of them standing outside his shop, the trader went to them and offered his respects by bowing to them. Both promptly asked him who out of them was more beautiful.

The trader was in a fix. He pondered over the issue and thought that if he declared Shani as more beautiful, Lakshmi Ji would get annoyed and all his wealth would go away and he would be reduced to a pauper. On the other hand, if he declared Lakshmi Ji more beautiful, Shani would get angry and if Shani's dashaa got over him, he would in a bad condition.

The trader thought for a while and said, while pointing towards a tree, "Both of you may please go up to that tree, touch it and come back, and then I shall be able to tell as to who is more beautiful." Both went to the tree, touched it, came back, and asked the trader, "Now tell us, who is more beautiful." And the trader replied, "Both of you are beautiful."

Both Shani and Lakshmi disagreed with this. They said that Brahma Ji had sent them to him so that he could give the correct answer. Then, the trader said, "Look, when Lakshmi Ji was approaching, she was looking beautiful, and when Shani Dev was going away, he looked more beautiful. Hence, both of you are beautiful."

The trader's intention behind this was quite clear. Lakshmi means "riches". When it comes towards you, it is good. Shani means "trouble". When it goes away from you, it is good.

Both Shani Dev and Lakshmi Ji were surprised at the wit of the trader and went back to their abode.

What have we learnt from this story?
1. Never make a mighty person unhappy.
2. Always make a decision after deliberation, and according to the circumstances.
3. Always bear in mind that both the above mentioned things are expected from you, as *this is what common sense is all about.*

15

Knowing Your Personality

Always be yourself, express yourself, have faith in yourself; do not go out and look for a successful personality and duplicate it.

BRUCE LEE

Our personality is our real identity. When we talk about someone, we often discuss about his personality. We always say that the personality of so-and-so is good or bad. Personality, although developed by us, is the impression with which we are perceived by the society on the basis of our behaviour. Personality is our identity card. Whenever we are reminded of someone, his or her qualities start surfacing in our mind and his or her image appears in our mind. This image could be either positive or negative.

> **You cannot conceal your personality for long. Others can understand it by your behaviour.**

What Is Personality?

"Personality is the sum total of our internal and external qualities, which gives us a unique character as an individual."

Before proceeding further on the subject of personality, it is extremely desirable to understand as to what the internal and external qualities **are** through which a personality is built up.

External Qualities of Personality

These are the qualities which are visible to another person about us from the outside, for instance, physical stature, appearance, shape of the face, dress, footwear, hair style, expression on the face, body language, etc. These external qualities of personality are very significant, for instance, clothes well washed, neatly ironed, suiting your appearance and physical stature, a smile on your face, using the hands in a normal manner while conversing, exerting weight on both the feet while standing, no pan masala or gutka being chewn, body not being kept loose, etc.

> A simple question: If you are not aware of the internal qualities of someone, then who would you would prefer to talk to—with a person who is tense and desperate, or with a person who is standing smartly and is smiling?

For a mature person, it is extremely necessary to work on his or her external qualities. There is a famous saying, "You do not have a second chance to make the first impression". It is an important fact that prominent industrialists, motivational speakers, leaders, professors, and sportsmen keep a track of their external image. They have a specific dress code by which they are identified. They have a specific body language which makes their job easier. In cricket, when two players go into the field to start their innings, they neither have any tension on their faces, nor do they laugh loudly. At that time, they are completely calm and their face bears a serene look, and this is what is expected of them.

Just think, if a motivational speaker himself looks tense and dejected, will he or she be able to motivate others?

Let us see, by means of a story, what significance the dress has in today's world:

Blunder of a Sales Officer

A company once shortlisted four persons for the position of Sales Officers for the marketing of its product. The candidates had to come to Head Office for the final stage of their selection. This consisted of meeting the senior managers of the company and a visit to the client.

First, they had to meet the Marketing Manager and the H. R. Manager of the company. All four reached in time, and all were suitably dressed for the occasion. However, one of them was not wearing a necktie. The Marketing Manager asked him, "Gentleman, you have not put on a necktie. You were told that today you also have to meet a client." The candidate replied in a casual tone, "I do not think that this will affect my ability for sales."

Not expecting such a reply, the Marketing Manager got annoyed and said, "We are surprised at the way you think. If you do not have a necktie, it does not affect us, but it does affect our client. When you are so careless about your external looks, then what kind of qualities do you have inside you? We do not require your services. You may go."

> People are watching you and evaluating you, so it is important to keep an eye on your external personality.

Internal Qualities of Personality

In a personality, internal qualities play a very significant role. In fact, it is the internal qualities which constitute our permanent personality. There is a long list of internal qualities. They consist of our viewpoint, behaviour, conceptual and practical knowledge, art of conversation, time management, analytical ability, impression about the society and the nation, desire to learn, etc. Internal qualities can be divided into two subheads:

Good Qualities (Desirable)	Bad Qualities (Undesirable)
Positive attitude	Negative attitude
Clarity	Confusion
Politeness	Rudeness
Learning attitude	Happy with limited knowledge
Patience	Impatience
Working hard	Laziness
Firm determination	Weak determination
Good communication	Poor communication
Truthfulness	Untruthfulness
Self confidence	Inferiority complex

Kindness	Cruelty
Tolerance	Aggressiveness
Enthusiasm	Apathy
Praising with heart	Jealousy
Patriotism	Disloyalty

Study the above list of internal qualities carefully. You will understand by yourself as to how important these are in our life.

How to Build a Good and Strong Personality

A combination of the internal and external qualities makes up a complete personality. A good personality is not built in a single day. It takes a lot of time. First, you have to imbibe good qualities, which are followed by their evolution inside you. Ponder over the above mentioned external and internal qualities for some time and find out which of the good qualities are less and which bad qualities are more inside you. We can analyse this in the following manner:

1. An analysis of your personality done by you

Self-analysis is the first step in the development of personality. Though we may do this according to our individual capability, it is not necessary that our analysis is fully correct. However, if done with sincerity, it will help to a considerable extent.

For self-analysis, make two separate lists of all the qualities of your personality (external and internal, negative and positive) — a separate list for both. Then, allot scores, up to a maximum of 10, to each personality trait as per your judgment of its level. For example:

1. Positive Attitude - 7	1. Jealousy	- 6
2. Hard Working - 8	2. Laziness	- 3
3. Firm Determination - 8	3. Aggressiveness	- 5
etc.		

Now, sum up the scores for the positive and negative qualities separately, and work out the average from the total. You can make an analysis with the help of the following key:

Average of Good Qualities
5 or less — You need a lot of improvement
6 to 8 — A very balanced level; do not let it go down
9 to 10 — This level is the best, but take care that nobody should takes undue advantage of your being good

Average of Bad Qualities
2 or less — A very balanced level; do not let it go up
3 to 6 — Not an appropriate level; start controlling them)
7 to 10 — An extremely dangerous level and needs immediate steps to be taken, otherwise will produce extremely adverse outcome

It is my advice to all the readers of this book to perform this analysis. You shall not only be able to discover your real personality, but will get to know something undiscovered.

> **The formula for personality development is quite easy—Keep shedding off the bad qualities and keep taking up the good qualities.**

2. An analysis of your personality done by someone else

The analysis of your personality can also be done by someone else. If you think that someone else can evaluate your qualities better than you, then you can get the analysis done by that person. However, such a person is not easy to find, as he or she should know everything about you. Your personality analysis can be done by your spouse, teacher, sibling, colleague, your boss or junior, or an intimate friend. In this case, the description of marks shall remain the same as if done through a self-analysis.

3. Analysis of personality on the basis of success or failure at work

Make a list of those tasks which you have not been able to do till now. Then, observe as to what good qualities are required to perform those tasks, or which bad qualities are required to be eliminated. You will come to know which good quality you lack and which bad qualities you have in excess. You can apply the same process to analyse those tasks in which you have been successful.

4. Analysis on the basis of behaviour pattern

Take a close look at your day-to-day behaviour. Make a close scrutiny of all your activities — whatever you speak, do anything, go anywhere, meet anyone, etc.

Types of Personalities

After this discussion on personality, the question arises as to what type of personality we should have. Books on human psychology give various types of personalities, but here I will discuss the types of personalities which we face in day-to-day life. You can identify your own personality among these and identify its qualities.

Types of personality can be classified mainly into two types — Optimistic (which is expected of you), and Pessimistic (which is not expected of you).

Pleasing personality

You must have seen persons who are always cheerful. Even in a sad situation, the person will laugh away the troubles. Whenever you meet such people, they always indulge in fun and laughter, and exhibit a feeling of enthusiasm to live life freely. Anyone who meets them gets a feeling of happiness and becomes eager to meet them again and again. At the national level, ex-cricketer and parliamentarian Navjot Singh Sidhu is the most appropriate example of such a personality.

Whether he is in politics, or working as a commentator or hosting a laughter show, he always looks cheerful.

Royal personality

This personality often belongs to those who are at the peak of their individual career. They speak very little, with utmost caution, and behave in a very careful manner. While they have touched the zenith of their career, they are also very practical, simple, and down to earth persons. Such people are respected by others, and they prove to be role models for the society. Some such personalities are Dr. A. P. J. Abdul Kalam, Amitabh Bachchan, Sachin Tendulkar, Atal Bihari Bajpai, and Lata Mangeshkar.

Socialistic personality

Persons falling under this category always give preference to the country before self. They are extremely popular in the society. They organize people for doing social work, and motivate them for doing it. They choose varied paths, but their ultimate goal is social service only. Examples of such personalities are Mother Teresa, Sunder Lal Bahuguna, Rajendra Singh Magsaysay, and Anna Hazare.

Innovative personality

Such type of people always do something different from others. They do something new, which has never been done earlier, and about which nobody could ever think earlier. For them, doing something new is the purpose of their life. They do not thing in a routine manner. The great scientist **Isaac Newton,** inventor of Sixth-Sense Technology Pranav Mistry, promoter of Ethical Hacking Ankit Fadia, winner of the Nobel Prize on Micro Finance Mohammad Yunus, are few such persons.

Dynamic or all-rounder personality

My intention for using the description "all-rounder" is to reflect on a personality which moulds and adjusts itself as per the demands of time. Such a person, according to the requirement, makes alterations in his or her qualities, takes advantage of the opportunities available, and avoids any type of possible loss. In practice, such a personality is very difficult to find, but the professional educational institutions are trying to groom them. During the Mahabharat era, Lord Krishna was one such person who could perform Bal Leela (cheerful activities as a child) as well as Raas Leela (Romance), and also use his Sudarshan Chakra (the powerful weapon of lord Krishna). And, he also knew how to win a war without using the Sudarshan Chakra.

> "The business world of today is searching for people with an all-round personality."

Attractive personality

People in this category are successful in attracting others towards them. Either such persons are very good looking, or attract others by their talk. For example, film stars and models, by virtue of their good looks become the centre of attraction. Poets and comedians attract others through their elocution. The greatest advantage of such a personality is that they attract a lot of attention from others, so that whenever they say anything, people give heed to their words.

There are some negative types of personalities as well. I have highlighted them so that you observe if you have them in your personality and try to discard them.

Doubtful personality

These are the persons on whom you sometimes doubt due to their talk or behaviour. It is extremely difficult to understand their personality. Such people behave normally, but somehow you have doubts regarding them, and hence it is not possible to rely on them. To understand such a person in the true sense, you have to scrutinize his or her background and find out about their goals and objectives. Often, you have to judge their behaviour from the point of view of social aspects. There is a saying for such type of persons, "One who is a friend of everyone, is not a friend of anyone."

Stressful personality

Such people are always stressed. They carry negative viewpoints. They can never be happy, even when they receive the highest gains. They are in the habit of talking in a manner which displays as if they have lost everything in life. If you ask them, "How are you?" you will get a reply, "Just passing time," or "Life is going on," or "Carrying on somehow," etc. Let us proceed by enjoying the story of one such person:

Stressful Personality—Bhushan

There was a boy—Bhushan. He was very intelligent and wanted to become a Chartered Accountant. One day he met one of his school teachers at a wedding function. He told his teacher that he was preparing to become a Chartered accountant. The teacher was very happy to know that one of his brightest students had chosen a good career path. However, during conversation, Bhushan seemed a little depressed. His teacher asked, "Bhushan, You do not seem happy. What is the reason?" Bhushan replied, "Sir! I haven't become a Chartered Accountant (CA) yet, how can I be happy?"

A few months later, his teacher came to know that Bhushan had completed his CA. The teacher invited him to share his experience and motivate the current batch of students in the school. Bhushan addressed the students well, but seemed depressed. His teacher asked "Are you not happy now? You have achieved your goal to become a CA." Bhushan replied in the same manner as earlier, "Oh no Sir! I have not got a job in my preferred company so far. How can I be happy?"

Sometime later, the teacher visited a well-known multinational bank for some routine work. He was pleasantly surprised to see Bhushan sitting in the manager's chair at the bank. He was delighted to recall that it was the same organization where Bhushan always wanted to work. Now Bhushan was a CA and he was working in his favourite company, still, he was looking depressed. The teacher went to him and asked, "Bhushan, I believe now there is no need to ask you if you are happy!" Bhushan replied in the same manner as earlier, "Oh no, Sir! I have still not found a suitable girl to marry. How can I be happy?"

Bhushan's teacher got angry at this reply and said, "You can never be happy with this attitude. You are a stressful personality. You are not enjoying your present, but only worrying about the future, which is not in your hands. Happiness is not in the outer world of physical things, it's in your heart. If you want you can be happy even after losing everything and if you do not want, then even after getting everything you can remain unhappy. Change your attitude of being depressed due to the next level of desire. First learn to enjoy what you have already achieved."

Bhushan got a lesson. He realized his mistake and thanked his teacher for opening his eyes.

Confused personality

Such persons live in a state of confusion. They are not able to focus on a definite goal in life. They cannot take decisions on even petty things, and are always entangled in multiple alternatives to choose from. They are always dependent on others for their decisions. Hence, often they prove to be problem creators for others. In essence, such persons are devoid of self-confidence.

Good for nothing

These types of persons are those who always boast big, but lack any concrete plans. They do not have any intentions to do anything properly. Such type of persons only waste their own time and that of others. Persons newly acquainted with them often rely on them, but ultimately they suffer due to this reliance. These people are very smart, but extremely lazy in performing any task. It is always wise to avoid such type of persons. Let us understand such type of from this story:

The Worthless Author

Once, a loud-mouthed author came across a publisher. The moment the author came to know that the other person was a publisher, he started making big claims, "I am authoring a book, which will be a wonderful book. I am applying a lot of thought in writing this book. I do not write just like that, but do so only after a lot of thinking. Each word of the book will come out wonderfully, because I always think before I write." The author was talking without a break.

Suddenly, the publisher interrupted, "Sir, please tell me one thing. You talk so much, when do you find time to think?"

> "Never argue with an idiot. They will only bring you down to their level and beat you with experience."
>
> **GEORGE CARLIN**

Anti-social personality

This is the lowest level of the negative personality. In reality, such persons do not have a personality at all. Thieves, robbers, smugglers, terrorists, all come under this category. These people harm the society as well as the nation, hence they are considered as a liability to the society. Surely, nobody would like to become like these. Such persons carry a maximum of all sorts of negative characteristics. Not that they do not carry any good characteristics, but the good ones are overshadowed by the bad ones.

There is no end to discussions on the topic of personality. Personality is the base of any person. All persons exist with one type of personality or the other.

> **The biggest problem with marriage is that we love the 'Personality', but in actuality we have to spend life with the "Character".**
>
> **PETER DE VRIES**

16

Keep a Control over Your Emotions

A person who takes life's important decisions sentimentally cannot remain happy in life.

A big problem persists with all of us—when in sorrow, we tend to get too sorrowful, and when happy, we are too happy. Due to this reason, we often lose control over our behaviour. In such situations, the decisions taken by us are often proved to be incorrect. As a consequence, we have to bear immense losses or face difficulties which could have been avoided.

> **When you are happy, do not commit anything; when angry, do not react over anything; and when sad, do not take any decision.**

Often, while swayed with emotions, we take decisions which cause problems during execution. Why does it happen? Let us understand, with the help of a few examples, the significance of these emotions in or life.

Emotional State 1 (happiness)

The most beautiful moment of our life is one in which we are happy. We perform a task to derive satisfaction or become happy. Often, when we get both at the same time, our happiness grows manifold. When we are happy, everything seems wonderful and we wish to derive maximum enjoyment from this situation. At this peak of our happiness, we are unable to control our behaviour.

Assume that you are sitting in your office. A friend is sitting with you, who runs a NGO, and expects a donation of Rs.5,000 from you. At that moment, you receive a letter from your boss which carries a bonus cheque of Rs.1,00,000. The moment you go through the letter and see the cheque, you jump with joy, "Wow, A bonus of one lakh rupees!" You narrate to your friend how you have worked day and night for this company, as a result of which you have now received this bonus. And then, you say, "You were talking about Rs.5,000. You have proved very lucky for me." Saying this, you take out your cheque book and give a cheque of Rs.20, 000.

Look closely at this behaviour of yours. This is not a controlled behaviour and may prove to be a bad decision for you. Now, let us go ahead with this situation. You reach home with the letter and cheque and show it to your wife. She also gets very happy. However, when she comes to know that you have given away Rs.20,000 without giving a second thought, she is surprised and feels bad about your giving away such a big amount as a donation. And, after a few days, you also realize that you should not have done so.

Emotional State 2 (achievement)

Whenever a person achieves something, he or she not only becomes happy, their ego also gets inflated. They gets so engrossed in their achievement that they forget to give the due respect to others and may even go to the extent of insulting someone. Let us understand this important topic through this story:

The Blunder of Draupadi

This incident is of the time period when the Pandavas had established Indraprastha as their capital. Their palace was truly a magnificent one and was constructed by a very famous architect of that time, a demon called Maya.

After establishing Indraprastha, the Pandavas intended to perform Rajsooya yagna. Draupadi was very happy and felt proud of her magnificent palace and the ever-increasing influence of the Pandavas. In the Rajsooya yagna, Pandavas also invited the Kauravas to participate. Seeing the grandeur of the palace, Duryodhana was astonished. The special feature of that palace was that the place where a pond appeared was in reality a floor, and where there seemed a floor, it was in reality a pond.

This illusion caused some trouble to Duryodhana. At one place, where he thought it was a pond, he lifted his robes and put his foot, but was surprised to find a floor there. Where there was a pond, he though it to was a floor, and fell into the water. When he fell, Draupadi, who was watching him from a balcony, gave out a loud laugh and said, "Blind son of a blind father!" Uttering this in the wake of her happiness and pride, she did not even think as to what she was saying, and to whom. There was no fault of Draupadi in whatever happened to Duryodhana. It could have happened to anybody visiting the palace for the first time. But with her rude comment, Draupadi not only insulted Duryodhana, who was elder to her, but also insulted her father-in-law Dhritarashtra, who was blind. Duryodhana could not bear the insult meted out to himself and his father. This single mistake of Draupadi increased the ill-will of Duryodhana manifold, and this ill-will resulted in causing the Mahabharata war.

Emotional State 3 (anger)

Anger is the greatest enemy of humans. It represents the negative aspect of our emotions. Anger is a part of a person's nature, and is present in everyone. Some people are able to control it, and some not.

There can be many reasons for getting angry — for instance, if even after a lot of explanations your junior is not able to perform the task properly, or if your boss has scolded you, or if you are a student and have been reprimanded by your teacher, or, even after a great deal of effort, your work is not getting done, etc.

When Angry, What Do You Do?

When angry, often people tend to throw things lying around, shout at a person who is nearby, take an extremely harsh decision, etc. On this, it is often said,

> **Any act performed during anger ends up in remorse.**

A situation of anger is very harmful for you, as it makes you take a decision which can harm you or another person.

How to Control Anger

The oldest method of anger control is, -when in anger, before doing or saying anything, count slowly up to 10. This counting takes a little time, and in the meanwhile your anger will simmer down a bit. This is a good method to control anger. Apart from this, you can control anger by the following actions:

1. When in anger, start thinking that *this is the most negative image of my personality*. If I am unable to exert control upon myself, it means that some part or the other of my personality is weak, and I have to make it strong.

2. We can learn to control anger by *studying the lives of great personalities*. For example, the wife of the great philosopher Socrates was a very ungrateful person, but he never vented his anger upon her, and always engaged himself in his work. Lord Krishna in Mahabharat was insulted by Duryodhan, Jarasandh, Shishupal, and many more people, but Krishna never wasted his energy by displaying his anger.

3. *Keep some material around which is able to help you to control your anger*. Whenever I get very angry, I look at the smiling photograph of my one-year old son Aarav on my mobile phone, and my anger vanishes. You can put a photograph, a mantra or a useful quotation in your office, house, or study table. Whenever you are angry, think about those whom you love, or who are liked by everybody, or who care for you. By doing so, it becomes very easy to control anger.

> **Holding on to anger is like grasping a hot coal with intent of throwing it at someone else; you are the one getting burned.**
> **GAUTAM BUDDHA**

Emotional State 4 (hopelessness or tension)

To get depressed is human nature. When we receive a bad news, we tend to get sad. When we suffer a loss, we get sad, start getting wrong ideas, and then we get tense. Often, we are so tense that we commit something wrong. Hence, when feeling hopeless or tense, give yourself some time. You have to accept the fact that everything cannot go on smoothly in life. Ups and downs do keep coming. While feeling hopeless, do not turn away from anyone, do not change the course of your target, and do not withdraw from the world. Never take a decision while in a state of hopelessness or tension. Divert your attention from that particular problem, and do something which may remove your mental fatigue. You will feel much better.

Let us understand, through a story, how we can come out of the darkness of hopelessness and light a lamp of hope, which can enlighten your life.

The Trader and the Yogi

A trader suffered huge business losses. He paid off all his dues by selling off his entire belongings. However, he could not bear to see his family in such huge sorrow, and was completely shattered. He decided to commit suicide, and for doing so, reached the railway station and waited for a train to arrive.

He was standing very near the railway track. A yogi was also sitting nearby, who could make out by the gestures of the trader that he was going to commit suicide. So, the moment the train arrived, and the trader attempted to jump in front of the train, the yogi held him from behind. The trader tried his best to free himself from the clutches of the yogi, but the latter's grasp was very strong. Only when the train departed did the yogi released the trader. Hearing the commotion, some people gathered at the spot. The trader shouted at the yogi and said, "What was the need to save me? You should mind your own business."

The yogi smilingly replied, "Brother, I have not saved you from dying. Even then, if you want to die, it is your own sweet will. I only saved you because you do not even know how to die properly." The trader again asked in anger, "And how is that?"

The yogi explained, "Look, the train under which you wanted to slip was a passenger train—a train with low speed. What if you did not die? Think of the agony which would have followed. Within half an hour an express train is arriving, which will be most suitable for you. Please do not get angry, and sit down with me. I will help you in attaining death."

The trader, with a disturbed feeling, sat with the yogi. The yogi, in order to spend time, started talking with him. He asked the trader about his family, children, and so on. The trader kept replying to all the questions. The trader told the yogi that it was his father who had started business, and after his death he had taken over. For a few years everything went off well, but suddenly losses occurred to such an extent that he had to close his business. And today, he was penniless. That was the reason that he was going to commit suicide.

The yogi asked, "Tell me, with how much capital did you father start the business?" The trader replied that he had nothing at all. To this, the yogi asked, "Then why did he not commit suicide?"

Hearing this question, the trader grew angry, and said, "Are you mad? Why would my father have committed suicide? He had the responsibility of my mother and the children. He was a hard worker. Every morning and evening he would teach us the accounting for business, and it was by hard work that his business grew."

The yogi put his hand on the trader's shoulder, and said, "O good man, you also have the responsibility of your family on your shoulders. You can also do whatever your father did. So, why are you going to commit suicide?"

These words touched his heart and made a big impact on the trader. He started crying bitterly. He thanked the yogi profusely for the explanation which had opened his eyes. He abandoned the idea of committing suicide, and proceeded towards his home with a new vigour.

Whether good or bad, time always passes. Hence, we must keep a control over our emotions use our abilities and take advantage of our qualities.

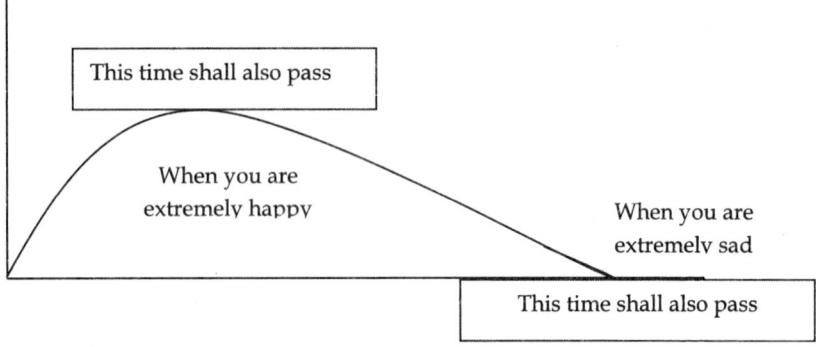

> **One who does not get happy in times of happiness and does not get disturbed in times of sorrow is a stable personality.**
>
> **SRIMAD BHAGVAD GITA**

17
Manage Your Stress

God never gives you anything you can't handle, so don't worry.

Osho once said, "Death is not a truth." Likewise, tension is also not a truth. Our happiness is in our hands. The scriptures say, "Eat only half, drink twice as much, and laugh four times more." In other words, laughing and being tension-free is far more important than eating and drinking.

Tension is a word used frequently in our lives. Every person seems to be tense. Whenever you come across a problem, face it with a positive attitude and this will help in solving the problem faster.

> **If you have to do something, you can do it either happily or sorrowfully. If you do it happily, the quality of result will be much better.**

A learned person has expressed life beautifully, *"Life is like an ice cream. Enjoy it before it melts away."* Those who perceive only tension in their lives, allow their lives melt away.

If you feel that life contains happiness, happiness will be there. If you do not feel that way, happiness will not be there. Happiness and despair are your own interpretations only. A famous Hindi poet has termed life as a struggle. Recall that in olden days, when a battle was declared, the brave soldiers were filled with joy, as they had no fear of death. *The most appropriate synonym for life is struggle.* If we have one hundred reasons to get tense, at the same time we have a thousand reasons to be happy.

Learned persons from the West have aptly described a smile as "Smile is the Universal Language." For all things in the world, there could be a thousand interpretations, but for a smile there is only one meaning and that is, being happy and enjoying life.

Life is a struggle, and we have to enjoy it, too. Often these two expressions may seem to contradict each other, but this is the actual definition of life.

> **One who learns to derive pleasure from struggles of life, whether big or small, is able to drive away tension as well.**

There is no denial that problems come in life. However, this does not mean that we develop tension due to them, and sit down in despair. The reason is that we cannot face a problem and solve it properly while we are tense. We can solve the problem better while we are tension free. If we get scared due to a problem and change our course of action, we are bound to face a loss.

> **Fear is embedded in human nature. But every kind of fear need not be due to a proper reason. If you have carried on with that fear in the form of tension, it shall destroy you one day.**

Managing Tension

There are many ways to live a tension free life. Lord Krishna, in Bhagwad Gita, tells Arjun that he only control his karma, and not the results, and that he should carry on with his task. Krishna explained, saying *Yogah karmasu kaushalam,* that is, *doing your deeds with expertise results in Yoga, that is, union with the Absolute (Paramatma).*

The above teaching makes it clear that the only way to reach the Paramatma is to *keep doing your tasks skillfully.* This we can never do while we are tense. A few guidelines to be tension free are given as below:

1. Let go of the undesirable fears

Tension creates many types of fears. We often fear those things which have the least chance of occurring at all. So, most of our fears are actually needless. Apart from these, there is no natural fear. We have created all kinds of fear by ourselves. Poet Dushyant has said this aptly:

> *Puraney pad gaye dar, phenk do tum bhee*
> *Yeh kachraa aaj phenk do tum bhee*

> Fear has grown old, throw it away
> Deem it as garbage, throw it away

Researches in psychology show that whatever issues create tensions for humans do not actually occur more than even 1 per cent of the time. You can now realize how much garbage you have accumulated in the form of tension. Throw out this garbage, which is there in the form of fear and tension.

2. Flush out the negative memories

Many of our tensions are our own negative memories. We keep getting ourselves disturbed by past failures. There is just one way to avoid this — *think that these did not happen at all*. Forget them and erase all things related to them from your memory. Do this physically as well, because, *whatever has happened cannot be changed now*. However, whatever is in your control can be dealt with happily.

3. Thinking too much will not help

Make life a simple affair. There is no real need to think too much. A poet has very aptly expressed this as:

> *Sochna waajib bhi hai laazim bhi hai*
> *Sochte rahna magar achcha naheen*

> It is relevant to think, and necessary, too
> But thinking all the time is not good

Some people simply keep on thinking. It is, however, not right to be calculative on all counts. Living life is not a mathematical process, but an art. It is absolutely necessary to fill colours in life and find ways of laughing. Searching for laughter and smiles in every aspect of life makes you tread your life on a simpler path, and then, even big problems start appearing smaller.

4. Never think of yourself as a small person

No person must think himself or herself as small. God has made us humans and given such a treasure of powers so that we are smaller to none. We simply have to explore and hone the qualities that lie within us. There is a famous saying in the business world, *Success has a simple formula – Do your best so that people should like it.* Just try your level best, and have a confidence that you can do it.

> **There is no word which cannot be converted into a mantra, there is no root of a tree which does not contain a medicine, there is no person who is not capable, the only difficult job is that of one who binds together.**
>
> **SHUKRACHARYA**

5. Do not have expectations from others

One of the main reasons for our getting tense is that we have expectations from others. We will have to change this. Someone has rightly said, "Expect less; you will be less frustrated", meaning that when you expect less from others, and that when they do not prove to be helpful, you will not feel tense. If you expect more, and others do not prove to be helpful, you shall feel more tensed.

6. Serve selflessly

If you wish to derive the maximum possible bliss, serve someone selflessly. Make sacrifice for someone. You will not get bliss greater than this, ever. After this sacrifice, nothing but pure bliss remains in your mind, and you will forget everything else. This is so because you are not expecting anything in return, hence the possibility of becoming tense will decrease to the lowest. By helping others, you also grow mentally strong yourself. You feel that even God is with you, as you are performing a noble deed. Dr. Kunwar Bechain has rightly said so in the following couplet:

Tumhare dil ki chubhan bhi zaroor kam hogi
Tum kisee ke paanv se kaanta nikal kar dekho

When you take out thorn from someone's foot, you will feel your own pains going down.

In order to live a good life, someone asked for three boons from God. If we understand these, we shall come to know the right way of living:

Someone asked for three boons from God:
1. O God, give me courage so that I can do whatever is possible.
2. O God, give me patience so that I can accept whatever is impossible to do.
3. O God, give me intelligence so that I can differentiate between these two (to find out what is possible and what is not).

The biggest cause of tension is only this. We do not know what is within our reach and what is not. It is pointless to cry or be sad over what is not under our control. Whatever is possible needs self-confidence and hard work to do it. You can do it, so there is no question of getting tense about that. What is required is the intelligence by which you can differentiate between the possible and the impossible.

7. Do something which will benefit all

In the business world, the concept of *Win-Win Situation* is often used. This means a situation providing victory to both the sides. A good deed is one by which everyone can derive benefit. When we think only about ourselves, we tend to get tense, because then it creates an imbalance in the society.

When we harm others and work with a selfish motive, we are under a constant fear. There is a saying, *Poverty anywhere is the threat for the prosperity everywhere*. Hence, we have to look for the interests of others as well. With the help of a story, let us see how a bad thing turns into good when good for all is done:

The Sweet-Makers and the Saint

In a village, there lived a saint who was very kind-hearted. He was strictly against any kind of violence and fight. If a dispute occurred in the village, he used to intervene and would resolve the issue. He would tell both the parties that they may hit him instead of fighting with each other. People started respecting him very much by virtue of his personality. People used to stop fighting and settle down merely on sighting him.

In the village, there lived two sweet-makers, who had their shops situated adjacent. One day, they had a fight. Both started throwing sweets on each other. If one threw a laddoo, the other would throw a rasgulla. If one threw a jalebi, the other would throw a barfi. While both were fighting, others were grabbing sweets and enjoying.

Suddenly, they saw the saint approaching. At once the fight stopped. But they were surprised to see that the saint, after arriving on the scene, had started laughing loudly. People were watching in astonishment, and the saint kept on laughing. Then, somebody asked, "O noble soul, you never like any kind of fight and always settle them. Then, why are you laughing over the fight of the sweet-makers?"

The saint replied, "Look, both the sweet-makers are throwing sweets at each-other, and their anger is subsiding. Nobody is getting hurt, and the whole village is eating sweets. It is the welfare of everyone. Let such kind of fight go on every day."

Both the sweet-makers and the whole village started laughing loudly.

8. Behaviour (*keep a clear, inside-out image*)

A lack of transparency in behaviour is a major reason for tension. In the first instance, people tend to avoid talking straight and frankly, then either they grow tense later or quarrel with others. There is a famous saying, *Shameless frankness at one moment, and bliss for the remaining moments.* This means that while entering a deal or a contract with someone, be open and speak frankly about all aspects, even if he or she is your closest friend. This may cause the other person to feel bad, but shedding off shame and hesitation for some time and speaking frankly gives peace forever.

In essence, I would like to say that, in order to remain tension free, we simply have to focus on our internal bliss. We keep searching for things which are all the time inside us. Laugh a lot daily, give respect to others, do not expect much from others, keep yourself healthy, keep away from greed, and develop the inner attitude of donating. Tension will not be able to come near you.

Happiness is truth. If you are tense, then bear in mind that you carry one falsehood. Drive it away and get involved in your work. It is foolish to think solely about the result. One who does not allow tension to dominate on himself or herself can do everything in a successful manner, and can attain achievements as never before.

When you lose something, do not ponder over it; rather, focus on all that you have attained. You will see that you have attained so much, and lost very little. It is a simple mathematics to calculate—we cannot lose more than what we have.

The greatest wealth is our life. Do you really want to lose out on even a single moment of your life in exchange of a physical article? Definitely not. So, smile and throw away the garbage of all kind of fears and tensions from your heart, and be free!

18

The Basic Mantra of Success — Time Management

Lack of direction, not lack of time, is the problem.
We all have twenty-four hour days.

ZIG ZIGLAR

There are many popular sayings about time management. It is said that everything is a slave of time, time is the strongest one, time once lost never comes back, and time is more valuable than money, etc.

All these sayings indicate the significance of time management in our life. Today, in the era of competition, time management has grown so important that one cannot avoid it. Without good management of time, success is difficult, rather impossible to achieve.

> **Time is our greatest asset.**
> **Losing it is the most foolish act.**

Time is our asset, but we have no control over it as it keeps on spending itself. Just think, if you sit idle for 24 hours during the day, can you ask God for 48 hours for the coming day? Never! Because even God cannot give back the time you have lost. Hence, each moment of time carries value. We have to take advantage of it and never to let it go waste.

The amount of time available is the same for everyone — 24 hours in a day. But, you must have seen that some persons perform a lot of tasks within this time and some find it difficult to perform even a few tasks. Some reach the pinnacle of success, while others earn their daily bread with great difficulty. What is the reason for this? The author of the world famous book on time management *Eat that Frog*, Brian Tracy says:

"We spend 80% time on those issues which have a mere 20% significance in our lives."

This means a misuse of time. It is very important for us to know where we spend our time and what we get in return. Let us learn, by means of a chart, the area where our time can be spent.

Order of Priority	Division of Tasks	Example
1	**Emergency Tasks** It is often very difficult to make plans for such tasks, because they arise abruptly, but need to be undertaken necessarily.	While getting up in the morning, you receive a call from a friend informing of his severe illness and you have to reach him immediately. Or, while in office, you get a call from your boss that the owner of your Company wants to have a staff meeting within an hour.
2	**Very Important/ Essential Tasks** These tasks, if not done in time, can land you into trouble, or you may face a big loss.	Reaching for a job interview, preparing agenda for meeting a client, giving a presentation in front of foreign collaborators, attending the marriage function of your office colleague or a close friend, students appearing in examinations, etc.

3	**Important Tasks** These need to be done on time. If not done on a daily or routine basis, they tend to accumulate, and this affects your very important tasks.	Day-to-day tasks of office and home, regular exercise, medical check-up, regular studies if you are a student, reading newspapers, getting regular sleep etc.
4	**Less Important/ Ordinary Tasks** These types of tasks need not be done at all. They should be done only when you have performed Tasks of S. Nos. 1, 2 and 3, and have time left.	Meeting friends, watching television, roaming outside, etc.
5	**Worthless Tasks** One should avoid doing these types of tasks and devote time in completing tasks of the previous four categories. In fact, these tasks are simply a waste of time.	Talking with a friend for long hours for passing idle time, gossiping with friends without any purpose, being engrossed on a social networking website or other websites, watching television for too long, sleeping more than required, etc.

Using this chart, you can categorize all the tasks you are doing throughout the week. You will understand which are the more useful tasks out of these, and which are not.

Strategies for Time Management

Given below are some strategies. If followed, I believe that *you can perform tasks worth 240 hours, in just 24 hours!* You only need to build them into your lifestyle:

Strategy 1 Perform goal oriented tasks

Perform only those tasks which serve your goals and those which are important. Do not perform tasks which give you short-term benefits, but divert you from your goals. Otherwise you will not be able to perform your routine tasks and those ones which are very important. Please bear in mind, you do not have much time, and if you spend your time elsewhere, your goal will keep moving away from you.

Strategy 2 To be able to say "No"

Often we do not wish to annoy people. Hence, whoever assigns a task to us, we always say "Yes" to it. As a result, either we are not able to do the task due to paucity of time, or we sacrifice our own important tasks for performing that task. So, before saying "Yes" to any task, always evaluate you own time. If you do not have the time, clearly decline. Otherwise the "Yes" can be a source of trouble for you, and the person, whose task you are not able to perform, will get annoyed with you. So, it is always better to say "No" in the very beginning.

Strategy 3 Do not procrastinate

Avoidance of tasks is the most common habit of people. Often, you must have observed people and also yourself saying that a particular task can be postponed and done "tomorrow", "some other time", "after some time", etc. Some persons do not perform their daily tasks, and keep accumulating them. Later on, the pending work grows into such an enormous size that it is not possible to perform it correctly or, while doing it, the advantages which were to derive from other tasks or opportunities, are denied.

> **Avoidance of work is like using a credit card. You can enjoy it only till you get the bill.**
>
> **CHRISTOPHER PARKER**

The correct strategy lies in finishing the task immediately. Never postpone it for tomorrow, and do not accumulate.

Strategy 4 Erase worthless tasks from your routine

Realizing the significance and priorities, we have formulated a list of many tasks which are worthless for us. Such tasks come under the 5th category and they should be avoided. In fact, they are not tasks, but a waste of time. When you keep an eye on your time being wasted, you will find that you have ample time for doing the important tasks. This habit is the mantra of time management.

Strategy 5 Optimize the time between two tasks

We often get across a situation in which we get some time which is completely idle. If such a time can be utilized, our productivity can multiply manifold. Hence, utilize such time to the maximum extent. For example:
1. Someone is coming to your office to meet you. You have just finished an important task and cannot start

any new task right now. Hence, you are waiting for the person. At such a time, you can do all tasks which, when the person arrives, can be left in-between and abruptly — for example, reading some good article in a newspaper or magazine, scrutiny and deletion of old e-mails, re-arranging the files in order, getting up from your chair and pacing, chalking out plans for the next day, etc.

2. You are in a barber shop for a haircut, and waiting for your turn. You can make your calls during that time, check emails on your phone, or send some important messages, etc.

3. You are downloading some large files and it may take some time. During this period you can perform a task related to the computer, or choose any option from those mentioned earlier.

4. You are in a railway station or airport, or travelling. During this time also, you can read an article or do some planning work or attend to your emails. During this period, you can also entertain yourself, as entertainment done within limits cannot be called a waste of time.

Strategy 6 Determine your priorities

Determine the priorities of your tasks, and fulfil them in the same sequence as planned. We often tend to first do things which seem to be easier, even when our priorities are for doing the difficult ones. Consequently, our more important tasks tend to lag behind, and the less important ones keep on getting completed. If such a situation continues for long, we are bound to face trouble.

Strategy 7 Prepare a list of daily tasks

Many of our important tasks are not done because we do not note them down. As a result, sometimes we forget a few of them. I often prepare a list in which 10–12 tasks are noted down for the next day. Sometimes, all of these are done, and sometimes a few are left. The next day, I include these tasks in the list again. By doing so, none of my tasks can get overlooked and I never get a surprise that a very important task was left out.

Strategy 8 Learn the mantra — It is now or never — Just do it now!

Often we tend to avoid tasks which we do not like to perform. For such tasks, learn the mantra of *now or never*. If a small task has been left incomplete for many days, and completing it is not disrupting your daily routine, perform it promptly. This will give you an immense peace of mind and you will be able to devote yourself to the important tasks whole heartedly.

Strategy 9 Take out time for everybody and keep a balanced routine

Your time is neither 100 per cent for the office nor 100 per cent for the family and the society. Your time should be divided in a well-balanced manner, so that there is time for everyone. There is an appropriate saying, *Work while you work, play while you play*. This means that whatever you do, do it with full devotion. Do not mix up the time for your family, society, and office. A balanced routine is the basis of *work life balance*. There are different priorities as to how much time is to be spent on work, family and society, and this differs from one age group to other. However, we can give a general break-up as follows:

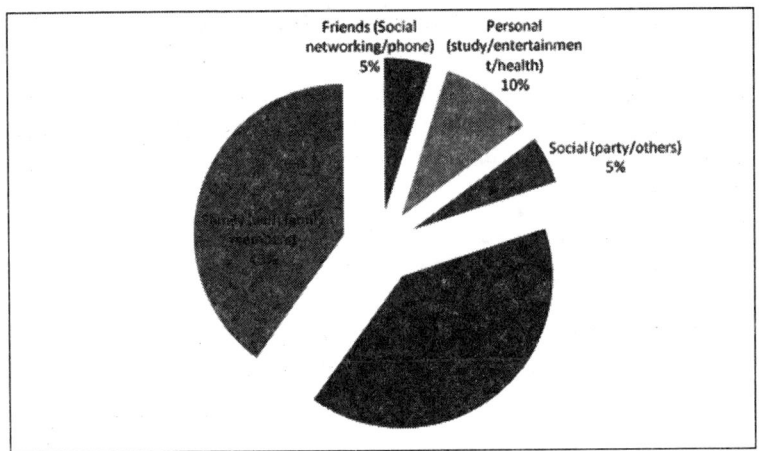

Strategy 10 Learn to take work from others

An intelligent person does not perform all the tasks solely by himself or herself. They *delegate* their tasks to other persons. *Always keep a list of tasks which you can get done from others, fully or in part.* You can take the help of your spouse, friends, and colleagues for many such types of tasks, which they can perform easily. This will save a lot of your valuable time and you will be able to devote it for more important tasks.

As a conclusion of this discussion on time management, here is a funny story about the impression of time carried by a simple man:

Laugh While You Learn

There was an idle man, who used to sit beside the road. Another person, driving by, observed him every day. He never saw that man doing anything and he used to sit idle all the day. The other person was observing this for the last one month, and used to wonder how anyone could sit idle just like that.

One day this person could not help himself and parked his car besides the idle man. He got out and asked, "Brother, I have been watching you since the last one month while going to and from my office. You keep on sitting idle. What is the matter?"

The idle man looked up very coolly and, waving his hand, replied, "Do not ask, this is a very serious matter." The person was not satisfied with this answer, and repeated his query, "Please tell me, what is the matter?"

The idle man explained, "What should I say? Many years ago, time destroyed me, and now I am killing time."

> **Being foolish is everybody's right, but some people often misuse this right.**
>
> **ANONYMOUS**

19
Be a Strong Person

When a person becomes stronger his problems seem to become smaller.

In this age of cut-throat competition, firmness is a strength and is extremely important for everyone. You have to face challenges at every step. If you get disturbed by these even to a little extent, you will not be able to focus on your path to success.

These challenges come in different forms. Often, you have to face an unexpected loss; sometimes people compel you to divert from your charted goal; and sometimes someone takes improper advantage of his or her position, etc. At such times, it is extremely necessary to become strong.

> There are persons who cannot scold their subordinates properly, and there are persons whose boss thinks twice before scolding them.

What Exactly Is Firmness?

There are many forms of firmness:
1. Firmness is — being persistent in the face of the most difficult circumstances and not abandoning the goal.
2. Firmness is — rooting out a conspiracy being plotted against you.
3. Firmness is — preventing anybody, then and there, who is taking advantage of you for his or her benefit.
4. Firmness is — scolding subordinates for their mistakes and making them realize that they did commit the mistake.
5. Firmness is — creating an impression on your boss that, before pointing any mistake of yours, he or she thinks twice.

This is the fact of life — when you meet a person for the first time, he or she is able to make out the amount of firmness in your personality. On the basis of this, they will plan the future relationship with you. *Often, people are on the lookout for someone they can fool.*

Firmness in some persons is in-built strength. These persons do not get bogged down either by circumstances or by people. There are many examples in history who have given a new definition to firmness. The greatest example is Sardar Vallabhbhai Patel, who, after independence, brought together 562 princely states into India, and made it a grand nation. Let us learn from his as to what a strong personality is:

The Steadfastness of Sardar Patel

Sardar Patel was a lawyer by profession. His principle was that an innocent person must be saved at any cost. Before taking up any case, he would study it very deeply. He would take up a case to be pleaded in the court only when he was convinced that the accused was innocent.

Once, he was arguing a case. This was an extremely sensitive one, and the slightest carelessness would put the accused in the gallows. At that time, someone gave him a telegram which only had his name on it. The moment he read the telegram, he grew sad for a moment. However, he kept himself under control and continued arguing for the case. After the hearing, he went out of the courtroom quickly.

Seeing this, one of his lawyer-colleagues wished to know the reason for his anxiety. Sardar Patel replied, "My wife has left for her heavenly abode. The telegram received while the hearing of the case pertains to this death." The accompanying lawyer said, "Such a big incident happened, and you continued with the arguments in the case? How can anyone muster such courage?"

Patel replied, "As such, my wife had died. How could I leave the innocent accused to be hanged? I did whatever was my duty."

We should not fall back from our duty, even amid greatest of perils. However, only those having firmness are able to do this and not everyone.

How Can We Be Firm?

Although firm persons are mostly so due to their in-built nature, you can also acquire the skill of firmness in your field of work and reach your goals in life, provided you follow certain behaviour patterns. Below are given some tips:

1. **Follow the rules:** Following the rules is the beginning to attain firmness. You become a firm personality when you reach your office in time, and follow office rules, despite being instigated by your friends to move in the opposite way. When you follow the rules, your juniors are automatically disciplined and they know that any breach in following the rules will not be tolerated by you.

    Your faith in rules acts as an example for others. When Dr. Kiran Bedi was the Traffic Police Chief in Delhi, she approved the challan of a car which was not following the traffic rules. The car belonged to the convoy of the then Prime Minister, Indira Gandhi. After this incident, Kiran Bedi was nicknamed as *Crane Bedi*. Think—how many persons have the courage to do such a thing?

2. **Be adamant for the right cause:** Always be inflexible over a correct issue. Many a time your boss, junior, family, colleague, friend, or someone from the society wants you to do something against your principles. Reject it outright and make it clear that you are not going to do any such thing, even if you have to take extreme measures. If you start being unbending over a correct issue, nobody will be able to coerce you next time.

3. **Finish your work within time, and get others to do the same**: The most important principle of being firm is—you shall finish your work within time, come whatever may, and others, to whom you have delegated some work, should also be made clear that you shall neither tolerate avoidance of work, nor any delay. Doing this will definitely make your personality a firm one.
4. **Talk less, and be particular towards keeping a distance in relationships:** There are some persons in the office who believe in gossiping and cracking jokes with all types of persons present there. On all days, at all times, they are engaged in humour with their juniors. By doing this, often they often have to face problems. The juniors do not consider them as their seniors, but rather as friends. And when these persons scold the juniors in the capacity of a boss, the juniors feel very bad about it, because by now they are now used to gossiping and joking with the boss. So, bear in mind as to who you are talking to, how much you are talking, what you are talking, and why you are talking.

    In the same way, you have to keep in mind about keeping a distance in these relationships. Do not have emotional attachments with everybody. Do not make friends with everyone, and do not try to build personal relations with everyone. As far as possible, keep to yourself, because if your colleagues take you lightly even once, you will not be able to prove yourself as a strong person in front of them.
5. **Face problems boldly, and solve them on your own:** Struggle is a part of life. Whenever a problem comes up, understand it in depth, face it and try to come out of it. Try to find the solution without the help of anyone else, till you are convinced that you have no other

option. Then only seek help. Even then, if you have to seek help, do it from selected persons. Presenting your problem to many people will make you an object of ridicule, because not every person is capable of helping you. And, if you seek help from everyone, you will be perceived by them as a weak person.

6. **Do not let others suppress you. Immediately say "No", or answer back**: The biggest negative point of a weak person is that he or she cannot say "No" to others. They always agree with others, and keep getting pushed. They feel that if they say no, or do not do the work of someone, then the person will get annoyed and walk away. In fact, the walking away is bound to happen one day. If you do 100 things for a person, and say "No" for the 101st thing, even then the person shall get annoyed. In return, there will be no benefit for the 100 things you have done in the past. So, it is better to politely say "No" to a work for which you do not have time, or if you do not have any benefit from doing it.

7. Another important point is, if someone is cracking a joke which you do not like, or if you feel insulted by it, do not tolerate it at all. Respond to it promptly and make it clear to the person that you are not going to tolerate all this, so that they may avoid doing such a thing in the future.

8. **Once a decision is made, do not make changes:** A firm person never changes his goals. He or she decides to do something after proper evaluation, and then implements the decision, come what may. They then neither care for accusations, nor the problems that come in the way.

> **The mantra for achieving a big goal is to hold it as a soldier holds his sword in a war.**

Be a Strong Person

Changing your goals repeatedly indicates weakness. Then, people perceive you as a flexible person who changes his or her course on facing the slightest hurdle.

Firmness does not mean being cruel, stubborn, or an egoist. This has to be understood very clearly. The points mentioned below distinguish between firmness, cruelty, and pride:

Not tolerating your insult is firmness, but insulting others is cruelty or foolishness.
Sticking to a goal is firmness, but giving up everything for the sake of a useless goal is foolishness.
Being disciplined with your juniors is firmness, but taking undue advantage out of this, getting work done by coercion, forcing them to accept your word — whether correct or incorrect — is cruelty.

Let us read the story of a Colonel and perceive the difference in greater detail. Enjoy this story but never be a person like this in real life:

Learn While You Laugh

A colonel in the army got married. When he took his newly wedded wife home, his dog, on seeing them, started barking. The colonel said to the dog, "Stop barking—one!" But the dog kept on barking. So the colonel said again, "Stop barking—two!" The dog still kept barking. Then the colonel said, "Stop barking—three!" When the dog still went on barking, the colonel took out his gun and shot the dog dead.

Seeing the incident, the wife got terribly scared, and said, "What is this nonsense? You have come home after such a long time. I am new to this house, so the dog will naturally bark on seeing a newcomer. You have shot the dog just over this small issue. You are not a human being but a heartless demon. Had I known this fact, I would never have married you."

Now, the colonel said to his wife, "Stop barking—one!" And the wife went quiet. There was no quarrel ever in the house after that.

> **The more you grow firm from within, the easier life becomes for you.**

20

Avoid Enemies and Also Friends Who Betray

A friend whose talk is sweet in person but who spoils the job when out of sight should be abandoned like a pot of poison topped with milk.

It is a fact that we all have some false friends and true enemies. Such people exist not only at the workplace but in the neighbourhood as well. However, most of these are often found at the workplace, that is, your office.

Who Is a Betraying Friend?

A false friend is one who always flatters you on your face congratulates you on your successes, and talks to you in a sweet tone. But, whenever you have any work from him or her, they make some excuse or the other. However, when they have to get work out of you, they will give the example of their friendship, and he can go to any extent in this regard. Such a friend proves true to the saying, "Honey in the mouth and dagger at the back." They speak evil of you behind your back, and can harm you as well. Every person has at least one or two such persons in their life. There are also false friends also who will never harm you, but they pose as friends because they need you for some benefit of their own.

How to Recognize a False Friend?

To identify a false friend, you have to adopt some strategy. To understand this, let us learn from the following story:

Five Friends

There were five colleagues, who used to pose as intimate friends of one another. One day, they all went to a jungle for a picnic. They wandered the whole day, and enjoyed a lot. In the evening, one of them suddenly fell on the ground and fainted. The remaining four friends started staring at one another. One said, "Bring the water bottle. He needs water to be sprinkled on his face." The other screamed, "Fool, we have only one bottle of water. If that is sprinkled over his mouth, then what shall we drink at night in this jungle?" The third friend said, "So what should we do? I suggest we should pump air into his mouth through our mouth, so that he gets up." And the fourth one said, "I cannot do an act of putting my mouth over the mouth of anyone, even if he be my friend."

They were all quarrelling among themselves, and not caring for their fallen friend. In the end, they decided that they would all return home the same night.

They were five in number, and the car could accommodate only five people in a sitting position. The problem now was how to adjust the unconscious friend. He could not be laid on the front seat. He could not be given more space at the rear, as others passengers would not be able to sit properly.

They all started quarrelling again. One said, "Place him between two seats." The other said, "Dump him in the dickey." The third one said, "No, let us bind him on the roof of the car."

Suddenly, the fallen friend got up, and said, "Do not worry; I can go while sitting upright. I was not unconscious at all. I was only acting to see whether you people are my true friends or not!"

Some Practical Tips to Identify a False Friend

1. Such people present themselves in front of you in a bit too friendly manner. There is a Bangla saying, "Ati bhakti, chorer lakshan", meaning that if a person flatters you too much, then he or she must be having something fishy inside their heart.

2. Your colleagues, or those who compete with you, can be your false friends.

3. If one of your old enemies, or one having ordinary relations with you, suddenly turns over-friendly, you should have doubts. Somebody abruptly extending a hand of friendship could be your false friend.

4. If you wish to test or understand a person, keep an eye on whom he or she goes to meet, who their friends are, what is their background etc., so that you are able understand their intentions better.

5. Ask for an emergency help from the person whom you doubt. If he or she avoids every time, then they are just a superficial friend.

How to Avoid False Friends

False friends are a hurdle in the path of your progress. Such people give you many assurances of help, and if you believe them, you are always betrayed. The most effective way to avoid such people is never to take them seriously. Do not get involved with them in any type of partnership or contract, or any type of joint venture. Do not share your secrets or plans with them.

Often, false friends want to take advantage of you. In such a situation, you should know how to ignore their demands. Do not make any commitment or promise to them, as you should not behave in a false manner. Simply disregard them, and try to keep a distance. In case their actions seem to cross the limits, you must make them realize this fact.

Good for Nothing Friends

There is yet another category of false friends, who are good for nothing. Such persons are of no use. The specialty of these people is that they occasionally phone you up or meet you in person to discuss huge plans. Thereafter, there is neither any call from their side, nor do they work on the plans proposed by them. After a few months, they again ring you up to tell about yet another new plan, which seems even more attractive than the earlier one. They waste a lot of your time, and then do not do anything, or contact you for months together. During this process they extract a favour or two for their own benefit, from you. Such people are called "*Good for Nothing*".

You must be careful in dealing with such people. Whenever you receive their call, either do not attend it or disconnect the same. If you have to talk, talk in brief. Whenever they start talking about some kind of a plan, tell

Avoid Enemies and Also Friends Who Betray

them clearly that you are extremely busy and will not be able to undertake any such project. By doing so, you will save precious time by avoiding a time-wasting discussion, and you will also be saved from making any promises against your interests.

Till now, we have discussed regarding dealing with false friends. Now we shall come to the topic of dealing with true enemies and how to deal with them. Just like false friends, you have to learn to recognize your true enemies.

> **A false friend and a true enemy, both are harmful. One is a snake inside your arm and the other is a python lying in the front.**

Who Is a True Enemy?

A true enemy is one who considers you as an enemy and intends to harm you. More often than not, you are unable to recognize such enemies. Hence, it is vital to learn to recognize them. The good thing is that it is not difficult to recognize them, as they often express openly that they are your enemies and that whenever an opportunity is at hand, they are going to harm you.

How to Deal with True Enemies

1. Collect information regarding the strengths and weaknesses of your enemy.
2. Contemplate on their friends, relatives, rank, position, and why they happen to be your enemy, and then make an analysis of the facts so gathered.
3. Never talk of them to others, but if someone mentions them, keep your ears open. However, pretend that you are not interested in that particular person.
4. Keep your entire information secret — especially from all those who have may have dealings with your enemy — direct or indirect. These secrets can reach your enemy.

5. Always keep one strategy of defence open for yourself—keep information on what could be the intensity of the enemy's hit, and what type of attack or power can be used to counter it.
6. Your power to defend yourself from a true enemy will be a true friend, for example an officer of the company who can be on your side when you are correct and someone is trying to implicate you falsely. Or it can be your money resources, your family, etc. You have to decide as to which power can be handy in the specific crisis.

> **A friend said to another, "If you need me for some work, you can wake me up at midnight—but do not disturb me in the daytime, as I am busy during the day."**

21

Handling Criticism

Criticising others is a sign of negativity and getting bogged down by criticism is a sign of weakness. One should avoid both.

In today's environment, criticizing others has become something of a fashion. Criticism has a significant place in office gossip, meetings, and personal talks—in informal and even formal discussions. This is so because criticism is the easiest thing to do.

This chapter has been divided into two parts:

Do not criticize others

Do not be disheartened if you are criticized

What is Criticism?

In simple words, criticizing someone is to find faults in him or her. Though criticism is of many types, but the best type of constructive criticism is *summarization* or summary. The worst type of negative criticism is *evil talk*.

Summary means highlighting the strong and weak points of someone. A person who summarizes has no intention to talk evil of anyone or letting him or her down. This type of criticism is done by teachers and professional critics, and cannot be termed as criticism.

Another type of criticism is *severe criticism*. In this, a critic criticizes a person in an extremely harsh manner, unlike a gentle manner done in a summary. Such a type of criticism is done during a debate. This type of criticism done by people to get their relatives to mend their ways, and improve performance is termed as *constructive criticism*.

The third form of criticism is *evil talk* or *just some criticism*. In this, the person simply criticizes a person or an organization for the sake of it, even if the person or organization has not done anything—whether good or bad. An example of this is the mutual criticism in politics by members of the ruling and the opposition groups. Even if the ruling group does something correctly, the opposition always criticizes it. Evil talk is often done behind the back, while *just some criticism* can be done either in front of the persons concerned, or behind their backs.

Criticizing Is an Art

I am a teacher, and I am compelled to make criticisms. But, I always do summarization. When my students give their presentation, I start by highlighting their positive aspects and praise them for their good work. Then I tell them about their mistakes and explain to them that had they not committed the mistakes, their presentation would have been more effective.

A criticism done as summarization never troubles anyone and it helps the person in learning from the experience. However, the nature of relationship between the two persons is important in criticism. A teacher can make a summarization about a student; a person can point out mistakes to his friend. But if a person criticizes a colleague, or a junior criticizes a senior or points out some mistake of a senior, the other person is likely to get irritated.

Why Should We Not Indulge in Criticism?

There are two significant reasons why we should not indulge in criticism. First, criticism done by you does not remain a secret. Second, a criticizer is perceived to be a negative personality. No organization tolerates such a personality for long.

1. Criticism done by you will spread like forest fire

The first argument for not indulging in criticism is that any criticism initiated by you (if not done openly) gets exposed to the person criticized at some time or the other. And then, that person can create problems for you. So, never criticize till there is a real compulsion.

In the work place or office, it is a common practice to criticize one's boss. In fact, whenever someone criticizes his or her boss in front of a colleague or anyone else from the same organization, they feel that the boss will never come to know of this criticism. But this is not so. The news reaches the boss very quickly. In fact, all organizations have a very interesting form of communication, which is called *Grapevine*.

It is my belief that whatever you utter about anyone, 99 per cent of it reaches the person, even if you have uttered it to your best and most reliable friend. This is so because we are human beings and relish the *enjoyment of talking*.

When you criticize someone, especially when it is your boss or a senior person, you tell the person who listens to you, that he or she must not discuss it any further. That person, in turn, speaks to others, quoting you as well, and asks them not to discuss it any further. So, the talk then reaches two persons, then four, eight and finally to your boss, who you were criticizing. Such a thing can have disastrous outcome for you. Let us see how this can happen by means of a story.

Pravesh and His Boss

Pravesh joined a large branch of a private company as a Marketing Executive. He not only had an expertise in his field, he also had a very good command over English. Even with all this in hand, he had a shortcoming of not being able to hold back his thoughts. He had frequent discussions with his boss, that is, the branch manager, on various topics. His boss was a senior and experienced person, but did not have a good command over English. And so Pravesh used to often make fun of the mistakes committed by him on pronunciation and grammar. However, the boss never paid any attention to this issue.

Making fun of his boss's English became a habit with Pravesh. Whenever Pravesh had to submit a report to his boss, he jokingly told his colleagues, "You can give anything to boss written in English— he is not going to understand anything anyway."

This carried on for a year. One day Pravesh noticed that some of his colleagues seemed to be very happy. When he asked them the reason, they showed him their promotion letters, and told him that those who were appointed a year ago had now been given promotions.

Pravesh was surprised why he did not get a promotion letter. He asked the boss's secretary if any letter had been prepared for him, but the secretary said no.

Pravesh was very disturbed and decided to ask his boss the reason. The next day itself he went into the boss's cabin and asked, "Sir, I am sorry to ask, but I have heard that all those who joined this branch last year along with me have been promoted." The boss smiled and replied, "Yes, you have heard it right." Pravesh hesitated, but asked, "But Sir, I did not get the promotion letter. Why?" The boss continued smiling and said, "You see, Pravesh, I do not know of English as well as you do, so I have not been able to draft your letter. I am still learning English, and the day I reach your level, I shall definitely prepare the promotion letter for you."

Hearing this, Pravesh was stunned. He could not have imagined, even in his wildest dreams, that his comments would reach the boss of such a large branch, where people were often not able to fix appointment to even see him. He repented heavily about his actions. But it was of no use and he could do nothing but repent now.

This is also an example of *grapevine communication,* which acts as a fuel in the fire for those who criticize others.

> **Any fool can criticize, accuse, and complain, and most of the fools do so.**
>
> **DALE CARNEGIE**

1. A negative person will criticize often

Those who keep criticizing others are perceived as negative beings. No organization tolerates such persons for long. Whenever these persons criticize anyone, it is assumed that it is due to their own inherent limitations. No one can remain their friend for long, be it their boss, colleagues, neighbours, or friends. This is because when they criticize someone, the person listening suspects he or she may also be getting criticized in front of others in the same manner.

> **Whosoever gossips with you for others, will gossip with others for you as well.**
>
> **AN IRISH SAYING**

Let us see, through this story, how the business world of today perceives those who criticize.

The Story of "Two Words"

In an organization, the employees were allowed to speak only two words in one year. Each year, a day was fixed when the employees would say whatever they wanted to the boss in only two words. If they were unable to say anything on that day, they would get the opportunity only the next year. If anything was said in two words, it was considered either praise, criticism, or any other feedback for the organization. For whatever issue was mentioned, a solution was found.

In the organization, there was an employee called Madhusudan. Like others, he too, one day, got the opportunity to say something to his boss. He said, "Room dirty." Others also spoke about their issues, on different matters. There were some who kept silent.

The boss gave attention to what Madhusudan had said. When he enquired, he discovered that the room in which Madhusudan and his colleagues used to sit was, in reality, very filthy. He got it cleaned thoroughly.

The next year, as usual, everyone got the opportunity to say two words again. This time Madhusudan said, "A.C. faulty." The boss immediately checked and found that the A.C. in the room was actually out of order. He got it repaired promptly.

In the third year, Madhusudan said, "Salary less." The boss, on checking, found that the salary of Madhusudan needed an increase. He immediately enhanced his salary.

In the fourth year, when Madhusudan's turn came to speak out the two words, he said, "Will resign." At this, the boss shouted and said, "You, out of all, should now give your resignation. Since the last three years, you are doing nothing but criticizing."

Do Not Be Disheartened If You Are Criticized

It is often said that a person is criticized only when he or she has some quality inside. *When people start criticizing you, you can safely assume that you are progressing in some direction.* The famous Indian singer, Asha Bhonsle, once said in a TV reality show that once the voices of Rafi Sahab and her were rejected. You can well imagine that, if they had not taken the audition test, they would not have been rejected. However, if they had not taken the audition test due to fear of failure, they could never become such big singers.

Handling Criticism

There is no great person in this world who was never criticized, as they do a lot of hard work, compete with others, challenge their opponents, face hardships, and then finally become great persons. During this process, many persons get annoyed with them and start criticizing them. Let us learn, through the story of a great artist, easy it is to criticize, and how difficult it is to do actual work.

Story of the Painter

There was a young painter. He was learning from a great painter. He had a remarkable passion for learning. However, if someone pointed out a mistake in his paintings, he used to get very sad and disturbed. His teacher took great pains to help him overcome this, but could not change his nature.

One day, the young painted a beautiful picture and showed it to his teacher. The painting was so good that the teacher jumped with joy and hugged him. The young painter was very happy with the praise from his teacher, and asked what should be done with that painting. The teacher asked him to pin it on the main square of the city, along with a notebook. The notebook should carry a message that whoever found a shortcoming in the painting, should write it there.

Hearing the teacher's words, the painter became nervous. He asked if there was really any need for pointing out such mistakes. The teacher replied, "Just do whatever I have told you."

The young painter put his beautiful painting on the main square. Soon, the notebook was full of all kinds of faults. Someone wrote that the use of colours was faulty, while someone else wrote that this painting was totally useless and not fit to be put in any exhibition.

Seeing such a severe criticism of his painting, the young painter felt heartbroken, and he went to his teacher, crying. He said that he would never hold the paint brush again, and would leave painting forever. Seeing his condition, the teacher said, "I have not reached my goal as yet. You have to perform one more task." The painter promptly asked, "And what is that, Sir?" The teacher said, "Now you do one thing. Take a blank canvas, colours, and paint brush and the notebook to the same place and write message that whatever faults have been written in the notebook may be rectified, and a faultless painting may be produced on the empty canvas."

The young painter did as instructed. Two weeks passed. But nobody used the brush and paint at all, and the canvas remained blank. Slowly, one month passed, but the situation remained as it was. At last, the painter told his teacher about it. The teacher then said, "You really are a great painter." The young painter was surprised, and asked, "How come, Sir?" And the teacher laughed and told him, "See, you had prepared an excellent painting within a few hours. And, out so many people of this city, nobody dared to lift the brush and paint on the canvas, even for one full month. Now you tell me, which work is difficult—criticizing or making a painting? Anybody can criticize, but a painting can be made only by a talented person like you."

On hearing this, the young painter became happy. He thanked the teacher for changing his way of thinking, and got back to work.

One who criticizes is not great, but one who does actual work, is.

Making the Best of Criticism

Never hate those who criticize you, but lend a careful ear to them, try to find out your own mistakes, and try to remove them. When the criticizer goes away, forget about him or her, but start thinking about your own shortcomings and the manner in which to remove them. The person who points out your shortcomings is, in reality, not a foe but your friend.

> **When people throw stones at you, you turn them into milestones.**
>
> **SACHIN TENDULKAR**

Some persons always keep inspiring others to talk openly about their own mistakes, so that they can improve themselves. My PhD supervisor, Dr. S. L. Gupta, while preparing a brochure for a programme, used to ask my feedback. He told me to find the maximum possible mistakes, so that the brochure could be the best possible, without errors. There is a very famous saying by Kabir:

> *Nindak niyarey rakhiye, aangan kutee chhavay*
> *Binu sabun paanee bina, nirmal karey subhay*

Nindak, that is, the criticizer, should always be kept near, as these type of people make your inner self clean and pure, without the help of soap or water.